101 BEST WEB SITES
FOR DISTRICT LEADERS

Susan Brooks-Young

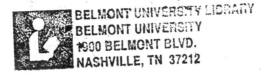
International Society for Technology in Education
EUGENE, OREGON

101 BEST WEB SITES FOR DISTRICT LEADERS

Susan Brooks-Young

DIRECTOR OF PUBLISHING
Jean Marie Hall

ACQUISITIONS EDITOR
Scott Harter

PRODUCTION EDITOR
Tracy Cozzens

COPY EDITOR
Nancy Olson

BOOK DESIGN
Kim McGovern

COVER DESIGN
Kim McGovern

LAYOUT AND PRODUCTION
Tracy Cozzens

International Society for Technology in Education (ISTE)
480 Charnelton Street
Eugene, OR 97401-2626
Order Desk: 1.800.336.5191
Order Fax: 1.541.302.3778
Customer Service: orders@iste.org
Books and Courseware: books@iste.org
Permissions: permissions@iste.org
World Wide Web: www.iste.org

First Edition
ISBN 1-56484-181-2

ABOUT ISTE

The International Society for Technology in Education (ISTE) is a nonprofit professional organization with a worldwide membership of leaders in educational technology. We are dedicated to promoting appropriate uses of information technology to support and improve learning, teaching, and administration in PK–12 education and teacher education. As part of that mission, ISTE provides high-quality and timely information, services, and materials, such as this book.

The ISTE Publishing Department works with experienced educators to develop and produce classroom-tested books and courseware. We look for content that emphasizes the use of technology where it can make a difference—making the teacher's job easier; saving time; motivating students; helping students who have unique learning styles, abilities, or backgrounds; and creating learning environments that would be impossible without technology. We believe technology can improve the effectiveness of teaching while making learning exciting and fun.

Every manuscript and product we select for publication is peer reviewed and professionally edited. While we take pride in our publications, we also recognize the difficulties of maintaining quality while keeping on top of the latest technologies and research. Please let us know which products you would find helpful. We value your feedback on this book and other ISTE products. E-mail us at **books@iste.org**.

ISTE is home of the National Educational Technology Standards (NETS) Project, the National Educational Computing Conference (NECC), and the National Center for Preparing Tomorrow's Teachers to Use Technology (NCPT[3]). To learn more about NETS or request a print catalog, visit our Web site at **www.iste.org**, which provides:

- Current educational technology standards for PK–12 students, teachers, and administrators

- A bookstore with online ordering and membership discount options

- *Learning & Leading with Technology* magazine and the *Journal of Research on Technology in Education*

- *ISTE Update*, online membership newsletter

- Teacher resources

- Discussion groups

- Professional development services, including national conference information

- Research projects

- Member services

ABOUT THE AUTHOR

Susan Brooks-Young has been involved in the field of instructional technology since 1979. She was one of the original users of technology in the district where she taught and has continued to explore ways in which technology can be used to facilitate student learning. She has worked as a computer mentor, technology trainer, and technology curriculum specialist. As a site administrator, she continued to place a high priority on technology and in 1993 founded Computer Using Educators' (CUE) Administrators Special Interest Group, which still serves as a network and resource for school administrators across the country and in Canada.

Prior to establishing her own consulting firm, Susan was a teacher, site administrator, and technology specialist at a county office of education in a career that spanned more than 23 years. She now spends her time working with school districts and regional centers exploring technology-related issues, developing curriculum, presenting workshops, teaching online courses, and writing articles for a variety of education journals.

Susan is the cochair of ISTE's new Special Interest Group for Administrators. She is also the author of the popular ISTE titles *101 Best Web Sites for Principals* (2003), *The Electronic Briefcase for Administrators—Tools and Templates* (2003), and *Making Technology Standards Work for You—A Guide for School Administrators* (2002).

ACKNOWLEDGMENTS

I have the opportunity to do the work I love with people I genuinely like. The staff at ISTE, particularly the folks I work with in Publications, Marketing, Professional Development, and Business, are incredible. Thank you all for everything you do. It makes what I do possible.

CONTENTS

INTRODUCTION

"Getting information off the Internet is like taking a drink from a fire hydrant."

—MITCH KAPOR, FOUNDER OF LOTUS DEVELOPMENT CORPORATION

Shortly after the publication of *101 Best Web Sites for Principals* (ISTE, 2003), district administrators began contacting me to say, "When are you going to develop a directory for us? We are just as frustrated by unprofitable Internet searches as site administrators are, and our time is precious, too!" And so, *101 Best Web Sites for District Leaders* was born.

The purpose of this book is to help district leaders become proficient Internet users and to provide quick access to high-quality Internet sites that district leaders will find useful on an ongoing basis. To achieve these goals, the book is divided into two parts: Directory of Internet Sites and Internet Survival Skills.

The directory itself is the meat of the book. In developing the directory for district leaders, I wanted, for ease of use, to employ a structure similar to the principals' directory. I also wanted to ensure that the arrangement of sites mirrored the structure of a district office. As a result, four of the seven sections in this directory are organized by the divisions commonly found in many district offices: business, educational services, personnel, and the superintendent's office. Each of these four sections is then subdivided into categories that reflect either the departments in that division or the special tasks handled by the division. The other three sections cover topics that pertain to all divisions: general, personal productivity, and social, legal, and ethical issues.

Please keep in mind that the sections and subsections are simply an organizational tool. District leaders in every division will find useful sites throughout the directory. Curriculum and instruction specialists, for example, will want to look at the professional development and teacher quality sites found in the personnel section. To assist you in finding all sites relevant to your position, each section begins with a short summary and a Quick Reference Chart listing the sites described in the section and their Internet addresses.

If you are just getting started with the Internet, before looking at the directory, you'll want to review Part 2, Internet Survival Skills. It will help you understand hardware and software issues and the ins and outs of Web browsing. More experienced Internet users will find useful information about advanced techniques in Chapter 3, Beyond the Basics, such as using more than one browser program, using multiple windows while online, organizing favorites, and structuring searches. The glossary in the back of the book will also be helpful to new users.

School administrators are increasingly being asked to improve their technology-use skills. You may find yourself using this directory, for example, as a text or supplement in a course or training on using the Internet. Leaders in many districts are also being asked to include a technology-use goal in their annual professional growth plans. Appendix A, which summarizes the National Educational Technology Standards for Administrators (NETS•A), and Appendix B, which relates all of the sites in the directory to the NETS•A, will help you complete coursework or professional growth objectives aligned to the standards.

Beyond this, however, my primary aim and hope is that the directory will be a tool to assist busy district leaders in their daily work. With this reference guide to Internet sites specifically aimed at your needs and interests, you will have one more resource to turn to in your efforts to create strong programs for students and a positive working environment for your staff.

When you can't find a listed site

Every effort has been made to ensure that the URLs and link names provided in this directory are as accurate as possible. However, Web addresses change and so do specific link titles on individual pages. Here are tips for finding information when a change has been made.

Typically, when you enter an Internet address and see something unexpected, it's because you've made an error in entering the address, so check that first. However, if the address is correct, and the page does not provide the information or links you expect to see, try the following steps:

1. Trim the URL by eliminating some of the information at the end. For example, if the address **www.ed.gov/about/offices/list/oela/index.html?src=mr** does not work, try **www.ed.gov/about/offices/list/oela/**, then **www.ed.gov/about/offices/list/**, then **www.ed.gov/about/offices/**, then **www.ed.gov/about/**, then **www.ed.gov/**, until you find a page you can access.

2. Open a page for the site and scan it for link titles or topics mentioned in the directory description. Sometimes the link titles have been changed slightly; for example, **Updates** may have been changed to **News**. Click on a title that seems to identify a similar topic, and you'll probably find what you are looking for.

3. Determine if the Web site has a search function. If the link titles don't look familiar, scroll through the page for a search option and enter the topic or link provided in the directory. This should lead you to the information you need.

There may be times when you enter the Internet address correctly, trim it several times, and still get a message that the page is unavailable. In this case, it may be that the computer hosting the Web site is malfunctioning or offline, and you will need to try again later. To determine if this is the case, try using a search engine to find the site, using the name provided in the directory. Follow these steps:

1. Enter the Internet address for a search engine such as Google (**www.google.com**).

2. When the Google page appears, type the name of the Web site as provided in the directory and click on the Google Search button.

3. Scroll through the results, and you should find a link to the page you want to access. Click on the link provided.

Sometimes sites go down and stay down permanently. The sites selected for the directory were chosen because they are sponsored by reputable organizations that have a good track record for keeping their sites current and online. If you find that a link simply doesn't work, please e-mail me at **Web4DLs@aol.com**, and I will try to help you find the site or its equivalent.

SUSAN BROOKS-YOUNG

Business

Educational Services

General

PART 1

DIRECTORY OF INTERNET SITES

Personal Productivity

Personnel

Social, Legal, and Ethical Issues

Superintendent's Office

Business

The business division of a typical district office often encompasses much more than finance and accounting. This section of the directory covers five departments commonly found within business offices. They are:

- **Facilities/Infrastructure:** Featured sites provide information about professional organizations that focus on facilities, the national clearinghouse on education facilities, air quality in school buildings, technology infrastructure, and a facilities-focused publication.

- **Finance:** Sites listed supply information about a professional organization, education finance data, financial requirements for federal programs, and total cost of ownership issues.

- **Food Services:** Featured sites present information about a professional organization, associations that focus on school nutrition, and the National School Lunch Program site.

- **Purchasing:** Sites include a professional organization for school buyers and a site for discount purchasing through the government.

- **Transportation:** Featured sites present information about a professional organization for transportation officials, as well as resources for every aspect of transportation planning, from selecting buses to safety education.

QUICK REFERENCE CHART

NAME OF SITE/INTERNET ADDRESS	PRIMARY AREA OF EMPHASIS			
	PROFESSIONAL ORGANIZATION	POLICY & LEGISLATION	PLANNING & ACTION	ONLINE JOURNAL
FACILITIES/INFRASTRUCTURE:				
Council of Educational Facility Planners, International (CEFPI) **www.cefpi.com**	▨			
DesignShare **http://designshare.com**	▨			
Indoor Air—IAQ Tools for Schools **www.epa.gov/iaq/schools**		▨		
National Clearinghouse for Educational Facilities (NCEF) **www.edfacilities.org**			▨	
NetDayCompass.org **www.netdaycompass.org**			▨	
School Planning and Management Magazine **www.peterli.com/spm/**				▨
Universal Service Administrative Company **www.sl.universalservice.org**		▨	▨	
FINANCE:				
Association of School Business Officials International (ASBO) **http://asbointl.org**	▨			
Education Finance Statistics Center **http://nces.ed.gov/edfin**			▨	
Federal, State, and Local Governments: Public Elementary-Secondary Finance Data **www.census.gov/govs/www/school.html**			▨	
Office of the Chief Financial Officer: U.S. Department of Education **www.ed.gov/about/offices/list/ocfo/**		▨	▨	
Taking TCO to the Classroom **http://classroomtco.cosn.org**			▨	

QUICK REFERENCE CHART

NAME OF SITE/INTERNET ADDRESS	PRIMARY AREA OF EMPHASIS			
	PROFESSIONAL ORGANIZATION	POLICY & LEGISLATION	PLANNING & ACTION	ONLINE JOURNAL
FOOD SERVICES:				
American Diabetes Association **www.diabetes.org**			▓	
American School Food Service Association (ASFSA) **www.asfsa.org**	▓		▓	
National Dairy Council **www.nationaldairycouncil.org**			▓	
National School Lunch Program **www.fns.usda.gov/cnd/Lunch/**		▓	▓	
PURCHASING:				
National Association of Education Buyers (NAEB) **www.naeb.org/membership.htm**	▓			
U.S. Communities: Government Purchasing Alliance **www.uscommunities.org**			▓	
TRANSPORTATION:				
National School Transportation Association (NSTA) **www.yellowbuses.org**	▓		▓	
School-Bus.org **www.school-bus.org/Home_Links/Gateway.htm**		▓	▓	
School Transportation News **www.stnonline.com**			▓	▓

FACILITIES/INFRASTRUCTURE

Council of Educational Facility Planners International
www.cefpi.com

ORGANIZATION DESCRIPTION. The Council of Educational Facility Planners International (CEFPI) was originally founded in 1921 as the National Council on Schoolhouse Construction. Its sole mission is to serve as a professional organization for people who deal with school building problems in an official capacity.

BENEFITS OF MEMBERSHIP. Members have access to newsletters, workshops, publications that target practitioners, and an international professional network.

SITE DESCRIPTION. The site is packed with information. Use the link buttons across the top of the home page to learn more about the background and history of CEFPI, regions served, programs and events, resources offered, and online tools.

HIGHLIGHTS FOR DISTRICT LEADERS. Be sure to visit the **Resources** area. This rich section includes information about breaking news and issues, research resources, print publications you can purchase, and links to other Web sites of interest to school business officials. The **Tools** section offers a searchable database of article abstracts going back to 1968. Full articles may be purchased for $5 each. There is also an industry job board in this area.

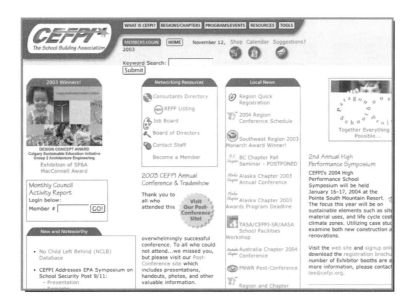

FACILITIES/INFRASTRUCTURE

DesignShare

http://designshare.com

ORGANIZATION DESCRIPTION. DesignShare is an international forum for architects, planners, educators, and facility decision makers. The organization has nearly 2,000 members, and the site is visited by approximately 20,000 visitors each month.

BENEFITS OF MEMBERSHIP. Although there is a registration fee for architectural firms that submit designs for the awards program or want to be listed in the directory, most benefits are free. These benefits include subscription to an e-newsletter as well as access to full-length articles and listings of architectural firms and facilities planners.

SITE DESCRIPTION. School business officials will find helpful information in:

- **Feature Articles:** Full-length articles going back to 1998. Articles are listed alphabetically by author. A sidebar identifies the most popular articles from each year.

- **Innovative School Designs:** Award-winning school designs from around the world. Designs are organized by type of facility and include in-depth descriptions and images.

- **Links:** An extensive list of links to other Internet sites offering information about educational facilities.

HIGHLIGHTS FOR DISTRICT LEADERS. Subscribe to *Educational Planning News,* a free quarterly e-newsletter. Click on the **Feature Articles** link and review the titles of the most popular articles. All are timely and useful resources for school administrators.

FACILITIES/INFRASTRUCTURE

Indoor Air—IAQ Tools for Schools

www.epa.gov/iaq/schools

SITE DESCRIPTION. The United States Environmental Protection Agency hosts this site, which focuses on the critical issue of indoor air quality in schools. Links include national information about air quality topics such as **Asthma, Mold & Moisture** and **Radon**. There are also tools for use by school indoor air quality (IAQ) teams.

HIGHLIGHTS FOR DISTRICT LEADERS. Click on the www.epa.gov/schools link to visit the EPA's new Healthy School Environments Web site and access online resources for a number of environmental issues. The **Get Your IAQ Tools for School Kit** link allows you to order a hardcopy kit or download all the files in HTML or PDF formats. The **Schools Publications and Resources** link points you to an extensive list of additional resources, most of which are downloadable.

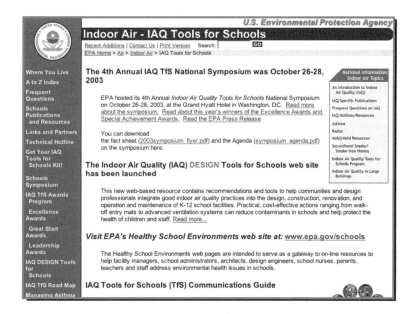

FACILITIES/INFRASTRUCTURE

National Clearinghouse for Educational Facilities
www.edfacilities.org

SITE DESCRIPTION. The National Clearinghouse for Educational Facilities (NCEF) is a free public service, affiliated with the U.S. Department of Education's Educational Resources Information Center (ERIC) and managed by the National Institute of Building Sciences (NIBS). The Clearinghouse offers information about planning, designing, funding, building, improving, and maintaining schools.

HIGHLIGHTS FOR DISTRICT LEADERS. Check out the **News** link for articles related to school facilities from across the nation. The **Resource Lists** link is a great feature, offering more than 100 subject-specific lists of online and offline content organized into five categories (planning, design, construction, financing, and maintenance and operations). The **Construction Data** link is a must visit for administrators costing out projects.

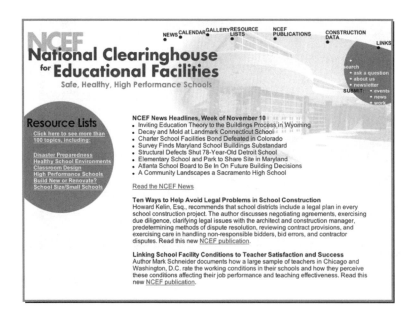

FACILITIES/INFRASTRUCTURE

NetDayCompass.org

www.netdaycompass.org

SITE DESCRIPTION. NetDay is a nonprofit organization that works to help educators make good decisions about technology implementation in schools. NetDayCompass.org is a directory of Web sites for school administrators to use when making decisions about planning, infrastructure, funding, and ongoing support.

HIGHLIGHTS FOR DISTRICT LEADERS. The **Infrastructure** section is an invaluable resource for school business officials who are called upon to make decisions about technology purchases. Topics addressed include hardware, software, networks, problem solving, special needs, total cost of ownership, and much more.

FACILITIES/INFRASTRUCTURE

School Planning and Management Magazine

www.peterli.com/spm/

SITE DESCRIPTION. *School Planning and Management* magazine is a monthly publication targeted at district leaders who make decisions about construction, facilities, business, and technology needs. Feature articles and special reports offer specific solutions to challenges in maintenance and operations, covering topics such as facility planning, safety and security, and financial control.

HIGHLIGHTS FOR DISTRICT LEADERS. The magazine's readership includes superintendents, business officers, directors of maintenance and operations, purchasing agents, architects, and state level administrators. Resources include an article archive, special reports, an events calendar, and success stories from around the country. While visiting the site, you may also request a free subscription to the print version of the magazine.

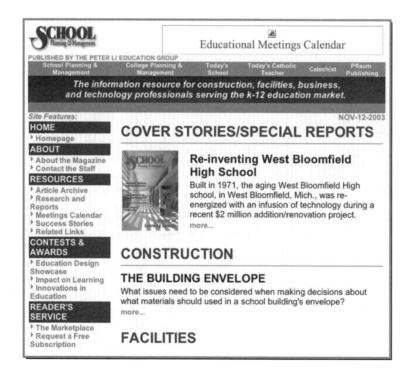

FACILITIES/INFRASTRUCTURE

Universal Service Administrative Company

www.sl.universalservice.org

SITE DESCRIPTION. E-Rate, or the Schools and Libraries Universal Service Support Mechanism, makes it possible for most schools and libraries to acquire reasonably priced telecommunications and Internet access. This site is the official source for all information related to E-Rate applications and reporting.

HIGHLIGHTS FOR DISTRICT LEADERS. The column on the left side of the main Schools & Libraries page offers links to an overview of the Schools and Libraries Division (SLD), as well as information for **Applicants** and **Service Providers**. There are also links to required **Forms**. Important announcements and updates are listed in the center of the page. Check here regularly to stay on top of deadlines and new information.

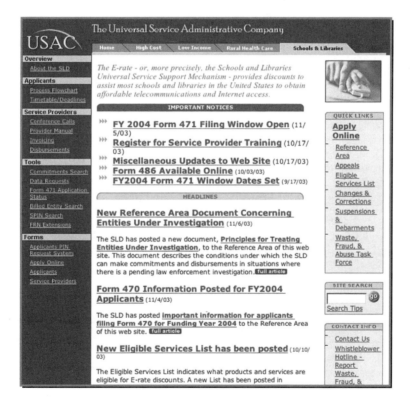

FINANCE

Association of School Business Officials International

http://asbointl.org

ORGANIZATION DESCRIPTION. Founded in 1910, the Association of School Business Officials International (ASBO) provides programs and services that promote high standards for school business management practices and effective use of educational resources.

BENEFITS OF MEMBERSHIP. Membership benefits include subscriptions to *School Business Affairs* magazine and *Accents Online,* a biweekly e-mail newsletter, as well as discounts on other publications.

SITE DESCRIPTION. The home page offers links to several areas accessible to members and nonmembers alike. Topics include:

- **Professional Development and Recognition Opportunities:** Information about awards made by ASBO, online professional development offerings, and access to **Web Forums** and **Online Mentors.**

- **Publications:** Links to limited-access archives for *School Business Affairs* magazine and *Journal of Education Finance,* as well as information about other publications.

- **Education Links:** Categorized links to education-related Web sites of interest to school business officials.

- **Legislative Action:** Information about current legislation and action alerts.

HIGHLIGHTS FOR DISTRICT LEADERS. Scroll through the entire home page to find links to tools and resources tucked here and there amid organizational announcements and updates. Join a Web forum or e-mail an online mentor to find answers to your questions. Check out the updates in the **Legislative Action** section.

FINANCE

Education Finance Statistics Center

http://nces.ed.gov/edfin

SITE DESCRIPTION. This site, sponsored by the National Center for Education Statistics, is a source of financial data for public elementary and secondary education.

HIGHLIGHTS FOR DISTRICT LEADERS. Do you need to know how spending in your district compares with similar districts, both locally and nationally? Are you interested in education funding levels in different states, or how districts are allocating their dollars? The **Graphics** link offers useful charts and graphs of national education finance trends. The **Peer Search** link allows users to compare their own district's spending with other districts. You can make comparisons with local districts or select districts from other areas; both options create Excel files for downloading. Visit **Publications** to order or download a variety of free reports.

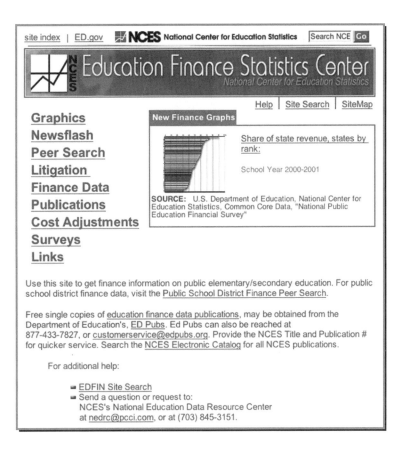

FINANCE

Federal, State, and Local Governments:
Public Elementary-Secondary Education Finance Data

www.census.gov/govs/www/school.html

SITE DESCRIPTION. The data provided here by the U.S. Census Bureau include information about the income, expenditures, debt, and assets of elementary and secondary public school systems. Currently, online data are available for 1992–2001.

HIGHLIGHTS FOR DISTRICT LEADERS. Information can be accessed in two ways. In most cases, administrators will want the annual reports that are available for download in Portable Document Format (PDF). Occasionally, there may be a reason for districts to download data files that can then be manipulated. Files of this type are available as well.

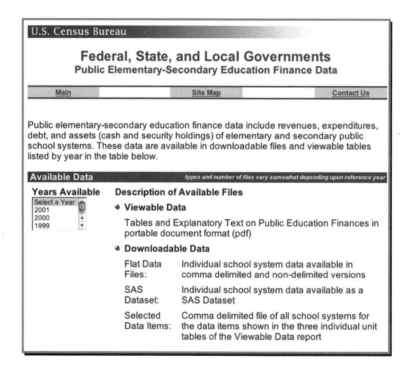

FINANCE

Office of the Chief Financial Officer: U.S. Department of Education

www.ed.gov/about/offices/list/ocfo/

SITE DESCRIPTION. This is the official site for the Office of the Chief Financial Officer for the U.S. Department of Education. From this home page, visitors can access information about programs and initiatives, reports and resources, staff directories, and news.

HIGHLIGHTS FOR DISTRICT LEADERS. District leaders in finance will find current information about budget forecasts and various aspects of financial management. Especially helpful links are:

- **GAPS:** An area where you can apply online for certain e-grants.

- **Grants:** A list of resources where you can learn about upcoming and existing grant opportunities, as well as information about managing finances.

- **Reports & Resources:** Guides, How-To's, and additional grant information.

FINANCE

Taking TCO to the Classroom
http://classroomtco.cosn.org

SITE DESCRIPTION. The Consortium for School Networking (CoSN) works to promote the use of telecommunications to improve K–12 education. An important part of this mission is helping educational leaders understand and provide for the ongoing costs of instructional technology. This site includes tools, publications, and resources that can help educators grapple with Total Cost of Ownership (TCO) issues.

HIGHLIGHTS FOR DISTRICT LEADERS. District finance leaders will find helpful information throughout this site. Especially helpful links are:

- **Publications & Tools:** Includes a guide for school administrators that explains TCO, a tool that districts can use to identify their TCO "type," and a Power-Point slideshow that can be used for staff, board, and other meetings to provide an overview of TCO.

- **TCO Checklist**: Explanations of the six major categories of ongoing costs.

- **CoSN/Gartner TCO Tool & Case Studies:** A tool for investigating the TCO for workstations, networks, and servers in K–12 environments.

- **Resources:** Additional materials about TCO.

FOOD SERVICES

American Diabetes Association

www.diabetes.org

SITE DESCRIPTION. The American Diabetes Association conducts education programs in all 50 states and the District of Columbia to educate families and school personnel about Type 1 Diabetes (formerly known as juvenile diabetes), which accounts for 3% of all new cases diagnosed each year. The site provides a basic overview of Type 1 Diabetes, as well as information and activities designed to help families and educators understand and support children in managing this disease.

HIGHLIGHTS FOR DISTRICT LEADERS. The Food Services Department is a logical vehicle for educating site staff and supporting students who are managing diabetes at school. Resources available in the **Type 1 Diabetes** section of this Web site include the following: information about dealing with diabetes at school; *Cooking Up Fun for Kids with Diabetes,* a downloadable cookbook for kids; basic nutrition information; and **Wizdom Youth Zone**, a special Web site for children with diabetes.

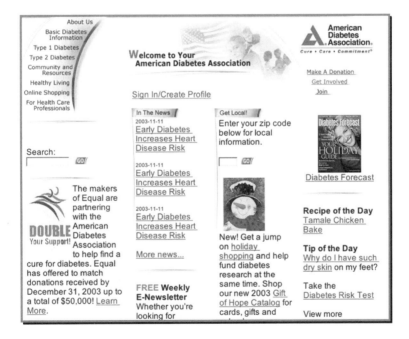

FOOD SERVICES

American School Food Service Association

www.asfsa.org

ORGANIZATION DESCRIPTION. The American School Food Service Association (ASFSA) has been promoting access to healthful school meals and nutrition education since 1946. ASFSA provides nutrition information and educational opportunities, and advocates for child nutrition programs in schools.

BENEFITS OF MEMBERSHIP. ASFSA members receive a subscription to *School Foodservice & Nutrition* magazine and can participate in professional certification and credentialing programs, locate and apply for grants and scholarships, access members-only areas of the Web site, and take advantage of discounts on conference registration and other products and purchases.

SITE DESCRIPTION. The site offers several sections that are accessible to both members and nonmembers. For example:

- **Newsroom:** Articles from *School Foodservice News,* industry-related articles from national publications such as *The New York Times,* and press releases from ASFSA.

- **Child Nutrition:** Links to a self-assessment tool for child nutrition programs, research on nutrition, food service operations tools, activities for teachers and parents, legislative information, and more.

- **Recipes:** A searchable database of recipes for school nutrition programs.

HIGHLIGHTS FOR DISTRICT LEADERS. Nonmembers may sign up for limited guest access to the ASFSA online community. Click on the **Join the ASFSA Web Site** for more information and the registration form. The **Child Nutrition** area houses a wealth of information and is well worth a visit.

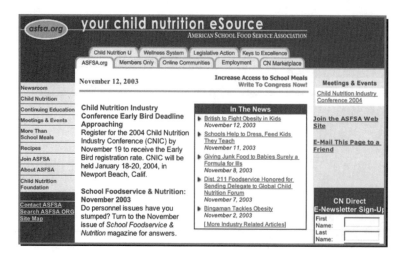

FOOD SERVICES

National Dairy Council

www.nationaldairycouncil.org

SITE DESCRIPTION. The National Dairy Council provides dairy nutrition research and nutrition education materials. The site is divided into three areas: **Health Professionals**, **Press & Media**, and **Consumers**. Contact information for local Dairy Councils (another resource for information and education materials) can be found in each area except **Press & Media**.

HIGHLIGHTS FOR DISTRICT LEADERS. Click on the **Search** link, and then type in school as a search keyword. The results yield more than 100 resources for school food service professionals. You will also find helpful information and educational materials in both the **Health Professionals** and **Consumers** areas of the site. Check out the **Links** to other nutrition-related Web sites.

FOOD SERVICES

National School Lunch Program

www.fns.usda.gov/cnd/Lunch/

SITE DESCRIPTION. The National School Lunch Program Web site, hosted by the Food and Nutrition Service of the USDA, is a handy resource for school food service professionals. The site includes updated information about **Income Eligibility Guidelines**, **Reimbursement Rates**, **Free and Reduced Price**, **Menu Planning**, and various food distribution programs.

HIGHLIGHTS FOR DISTRICT LEADERS. Click on the **What's New** link on the home page to access news updates and helpful tools, such as the School Breakfast Tool Kit. Much of the information here can be shared with site level administrators, teachers, and parents. If you're looking for research on nutrition programs, try the **Research** link, also found on the home page. The **Program Data** link, located just below **Research**, may have data you can use as well.

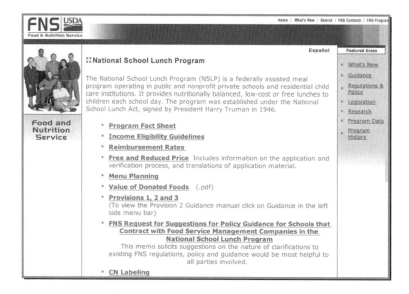

PURCHASING

National Association of Education Buyers

www.naeb.org/membership.htm

ORGANIZATION DESCRIPTION. Originally organized in 1921 to serve colleges and universities, the National Association of Education Buyers (NAEB) has been accepting K–12 members since December 2002. NAEB provides a forum for purchasing professionals to share information through networking and ongoing education.

BENEFITS OF MEMBERSHIP. Membership is institutional, not individual. Any employee who has purchasing responsibility may take advantage of membership benefits once an institutional membership is purchased. Benefits include publications, access to members-only areas of the Web site, and links to regional groups.

SITE DESCRIPTION. The site offers several sections that are accessible to members and nonmembers alike. These include:

- **Listserv and Listserv Archive:** National and regional e-mail lists for purchasing professionals.

- **Professional Development:** Information about various institutes offered by NAEB.

- **Archives:** Links to articles from past issues of *Purchasing Link* and the *NAEB Bulletin*.

HIGHLIGHTS FOR DISTRICT LEADERS. Nonmembers may sign up for 30-day access to the listserv. The article archive includes a number of items of interest.

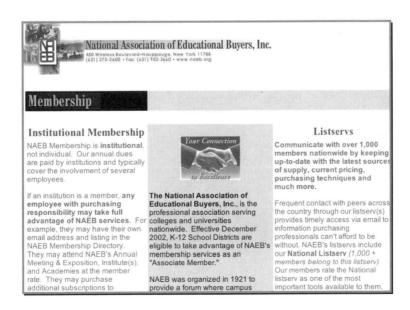

PURCHASING

U.S. Communities: Government Purchasing Alliance
www.uscommunities.org

SITE DESCRIPTION. School districts may purchase items through this nonprofit organization. A wide array of products are available, including office and school supplies, furniture, technology, janitorial supplies, carpet and flooring, and office machines.

HIGHLIGHTS FOR DISTRICT LEADERS. There is no fee to purchase through this alliance. Visit the **FAQs** link for general information, and then visit various **Product Categories** to see what's currently available.

TRANSPORTATION

National School Transportation Association

www.yellowbuses.org

ORGANIZATION DESCRIPTION. The National School Transportation Association (NSTA) represents companies that own and operate school buses and contract with school districts to provide transportation services.

BENEFITS OF MEMBERSHIP. Members receive information on federal Motor Carrier Safety Regulations, the *NSTA Newsletter,* research reports, and other support materials.

SITE DESCRIPTION. Although geared primarily to private contractors, school transportation officials will find helpful information using the **NSTA Information** link.

HIGHLIGHTS FOR DISTRICT LEADERS. Visit the **NSTA Information** area and review the reports available there. Current topics include occupant protection in school buses, the ABCs of school busing, and a safety guide.

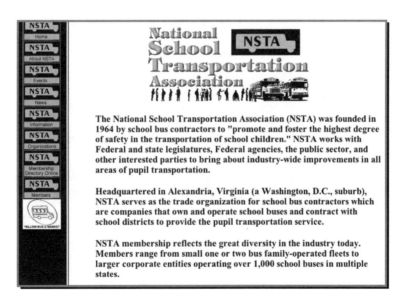

TRANSPORTATION

School-Bus.org

www.school-bus.org/Home_Links/Gateway.htm

SITE DESCRIPTION. School-Bus.org is a nonprofit organization that provides information about school transportation. A variety of documents, Web links, and articles are available on this site, which features information specific to the state of Florida as well as material applicable to the United States as a whole.

HIGHLIGHTS FOR DISTRICT LEADERS. Scroll through the Home page to see links to all kinds of resources. Particularly interesting resources are listed under **Documents (U.S. National)**, **Program Information (U.S. National)**, **Articles** (both sections), and **Laws & Regulations (U.S. National)**.

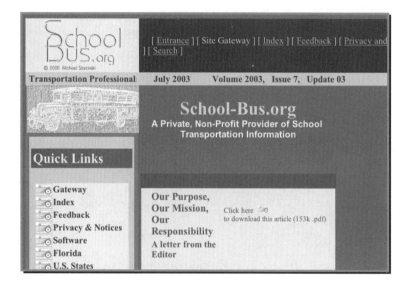

TRANSPORTATION

School Transportation News

www.stnonline.com

SITE DESCRIPTION. *School Transportation News* is a monthly magazine. The accompanying Web site includes more than 1,000 pages of information for school transportation professionals. While you will want to explore most of the links provided on the left side of the Home page, you may want to begin with:

- **Industry News:** Breaking articles about transportation.

- **School Bus Safety:** General information about busing.

- **Special Needs Transportation:** Specific recommendations for transporting children with special needs.

- **Government:** Information about laws and regulations at the state and federal levels.

HIGHLIGHTS FOR DISTRICT LEADERS. Sign up for the free STN weekly e-news mailing list service to receive weekly updates on transportation news. Visit **School Bus Safety** to access transportation data, position papers, and a special area for **Kids and Parents.** **Special Needs Transportation** includes a wealth of information about transporting children with special needs, including **Data and Statistics, Federal Laws,** and **Special Needs Links.**

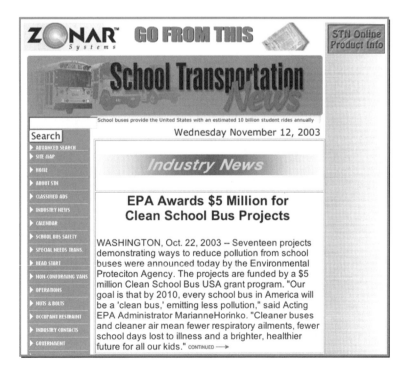

Educational Services

J ust as this division is typically the largest in a school district office, this section of the directory contains the greatest number of emphasis areas. These nine areas correlate with departments commonly grouped under the umbrella of educational services:

- **Bilingual Education:** Featured sites provide information and resources for planning and implementing effective programs for English language learners. A site that provides examples of best practices is also included.

- **Curriculum and Instruction:** Sites include a professional organization's home page, two databases (one for national standards in all content areas and the other for instructional strategies), and a resource for finding free instructional materials.

- **Early Childhood Education:** Sites include a professional organization's home page, a resource for free instruction and curriculum materials, and a site that explores the benefits and drawbacks of computer use for young children.

- **Grant Writing:** Three resources for grant writers include information about where to find funding and how to write successful proposals. One site offers a glossary of terms for grant writers.

- **Pupil Personnel:** Featured sites support district efforts in public relations, discipline, and school safety.

- **Special Education:** Sites listed here include a professional organization's home page and two general resources for information about special education. A fourth site looks at how assistive technology can be used with special education students.

- **Special Projects:** These sites address federal projects, adult education, and the school/home connection. There is also a URL for the Regional Educational Laboratories network. Each lab has its own area of expertise and at least one area of national emphasis.

- **Technology:** Sites selected for this area emphasize the leadership skills that district leaders must have to implement effective instructional technology programs. The Regional Technology in Education Consortia site and the Technology Information Center for Administrative Leadership site merit regular visits to review updates and changes in the instructional technology landscape.

- **Testing, Assessment, and Research:** Sites in this section provide information about assessment, student performance statistics, and links to research. The Regional Educational Laboratories network (listed under Special Projects) is also a resource for assessment, evaluation, and research.

QUICK REFERENCE CHART

NAME OF SITE/INTERNET ADDRESS	PRIMARY AREA OF EMPHASIS			
	PROFESSIONAL ORGANIZATION	POLICY & LEGISLATION	PLANNING & ACTION	ONLINE JOURNAL
BILINGUAL EDUCATION:				
National Association for Bilingual Education (NABE) **www.nabe.org**	▓			
National Clearinghouse for English Language Acquisition and Language Instruction Educational Programs (NCELA) **www.ncela.gwu.edu**			▓	
Office of English Language Acquisition, Language Enhancement, and Academic Achievement for Limited English Proficient Students **www.ed.gov/about/offices/list/oela/**		▓		
Portraits of Success **www2.lab.brown.edu/NABE/portraits.taf**			▓	
CURRICULUM AND INSTRUCTION:				
Association for Supervision and Curriculum Development (ASCD) **www.ascd.org**	▓		▓	
Content Knowledge—3rd Edition **www.mcrel.org/standards-benchmarks**			▓	
Exploration in Learning and Instruction: The Theory Into Practice Database **http://tip.psychology.org**			▓	
Federal Resources for Educational Excellence (FREE) **www.ed.gov/free**			▓	
EARLY CHILDHOOD EDUCATION:				
Everything for Early Childhood Education: EduPuppy **www.edupuppy.com**			▓	
National Association for Education of Young Children (NAEYC) **www.naeyc.org**	▓			
Technology in Early Childhood Education **www.netc.org/earlyconnections**			▓	

QUICK REFERENCE CHART

NAME OF SITE/INTERNET ADDRESS	PRIMARY AREA OF EMPHASIS			
	PROFESSIONAL ORGANIZATION	POLICY & LEGISLATION	PLANNING & ACTION	ONLINE JOURNAL
GRANT WRITING:				
Getting Grants: Finding Funding Sources Online **www.libraryspot.com/features/ grantsfeature.html**		▩	▩	
Grantionary **www.eduplace.com/grants/help/grantionary.html**			▩	
Grants and Contracts **www.ed.gov/fund/landng.jhtml**		▩	▩	
SchoolGrants **www.schoolgrants.org**			▩	
PUPIL PERSONNEL:				
The Behavior Home Page **www.state.ky.us/agencies/behave/ homepage.html**		▩	▩	
National School Public Relations Association (NSPRA) **www.nspra.org**	▩			
Office of Safe and Drug-Free Schools (OSDFS) **www.ed.gov/about/offices/list/osdfs/**		▩	▩	
The SafetyZone **www.safetyzone.org**			▩	
School Safety **www.nea.org/issues/safescho**			▩	
SPECIAL EDUCATION:				
Center for Applied Special Technology (CAST) **www.cast.org**			▩	
Council for Exceptional Children (CEC) **www.cec.sped.org**	▩	▩		
National Center for Learning Disabilities **www.ncld.org**			▩	
SchwabLearning.org **www.schwablearning.org**			▩	

QUICK REFERENCE CHART

NAME OF SITE/INTERNET ADDRESS	PRIMARY AREA OF EMPHASIS			
	PROFESSIONAL ORGANIZATION	POLICY & LEGISLATION	PLANNING & ACTION	ONLINE JOURNAL
SPECIAL PROJECTS:				
Especially for Parents www.ed.gov/parents/landing/jhtml?src=pn			■	
National PTA www.pta.org	■			
No Child Left Behind www.ed.gov/nclb/landing.jhtml		■	■	
Office of Vocational and Adult Education (OVAE) www.ed.gov/about/offices/list/ovae		■	■	
Regional Educational Laboratories Network www.relnetwork.org			■	
Student Achievement and School Accountability Programs www.ed.gov/about/offices/list/oese/sasa		■	■	
TECHNOLOGY:				
Center for Applied Research in Educational Technology (CARET) http://caret.iste.org			■	
eSchoolNews Online www.eschoolnews.com				■
International Society for Technology in Education www.iste.org	■		■	
Network of Regional Technology in Education Consortia (R*TEC) www.rtec.org			■	
Planning for Technology: Putting the Pieces Together www.edgateway.net/cs/tk/print/rtec_docs/ tk_home.html			■	
Technology Briefs for NCLB Planners www.neirtec.org/products/techbriefs/				■

QUICK REFERENCE CHART

NAME OF SITE/INTERNET ADDRESS	PRIMARY AREA OF EMPHASIS			
	PROFESSIONAL ORGANIZATION	POLICY & LEGISLATION	PLANNING & ACTION	ONLINE JOURNAL
TECHNOLOGY:				
Technology Information Center for Administrative Leadership (TICAL) **www.portical.org**			■	
TESTING, ASSESSMENT, AND RESEARCH:				
Brown Center on Educational Policy **www.brookings.edu/browncenter**			■	
National Assessment Governing Board (NAGB) **www.nagb.org**		■		
National Center for Educational Statistics (NCES) **http://nces.ed.gov/practitioners/ administrators.asp**		■	■	
National Center for Research on Evaluation, Standards, and Student Testing (CRESST) **www.cse.ucla.edu**		■	■	
Rand Education **www.rand.org/education/**				■

BILINGUAL EDUCATION

National Association for Bilingual Education

www.nabe.org

ORGANIZATION DESCRIPTION. The National Association for Bilingual Education (NABE) has more than 5,000 members. Originally formed to provide support for bilingual education, NABE now advocates for programs that support English language learners.

BENEFITS OF MEMBERSHIP. Members receive a one-year subscription to the *NABE News Magazine,* a discount on the subscription rate for *Bilingual Research Journal,* access to the members-only section of the NABE Web site, and a reduced registration rate for the national conference.

SITE DESCRIPTION. Much of the site is devoted specifically to NABE activities and products that may be purchased. However, there are links that offer valuable information for district level officials, such as:

- **Legislation/Policy:** This rich area contains information about laws, court rulings, bills pending in Congress, funding, and bilingual programs in various states.

- **Links & Resources:** Links to other professional organizations that support English language learners.

HIGHLIGHTS FOR DISTRICT LEADERS. Many of your legislation and policy questions will be answered here. Spend some time perusing the **Legislation/Policy** area to familiarize yourself with the various topics, and then return regularly for updates.

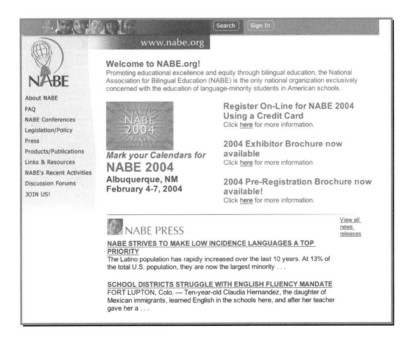

BILINGUAL EDUCATION

National Clearinghouse for English Language Acquisition and Language Instruction Educational Programs

www.ncela.gwu.edu

SITE DESCRIPTION. The National Clearinghouse for English Language Acquisition and Language Instruction Educational Programs (NCELA), formerly the National Clearinghouse for Bilingual Education, provides information about effective educational methods and resources for linguistically diverse learners. Visitors to the site will find databases, an online library, practical classroom tools, success stories, and much more.

HIGHLIGHTS FOR DISTRICT LEADERS. Subscribe to the free online newsletter, *NCELA E-News*. Past issues are also available on the Web site. Visit the **In the Classroom** area to find links to full-text resources of interest to leaders in curriculum and instruction. The **Success Stories** link offers a number of models for successful Bilingual/ESL program implementation.

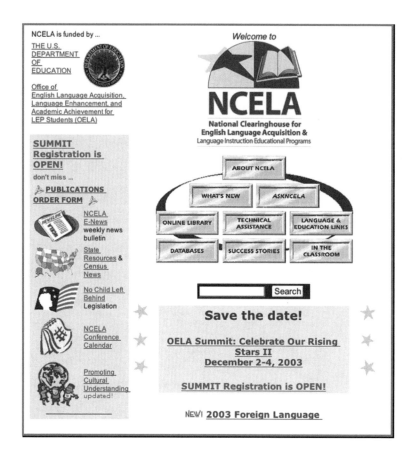

BILINGUAL EDUCATION

Office of English Language Acquisition, Language Enhancement, and Academic Achievement for Limited English Proficient Students
www.ed.gov/about/offices/list/oela/

SITE DESCRIPTION. This is the official site for the U.S. Department of Education's Office of English Language Acquisition (OELA). From this home page, visitors can access reports and resources, staff directories, news, and information about programs and initiatives.

HIGHLIGHTS FOR DISTRICT LEADERS. District leaders who are responsible for Title III programs will want to bookmark this site and refer to it frequently. You will find specific information about programs and funding, regulations, report forms, and much more.

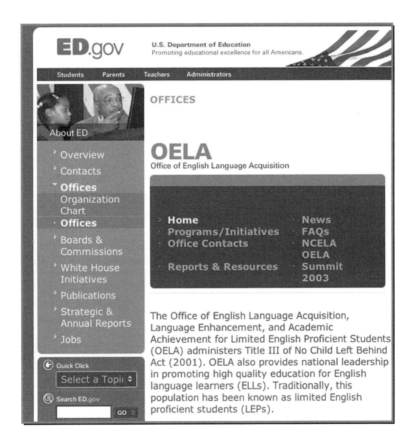

BILINGUAL EDUCATION

Portraits of Success

www2.lab.brown.edu/NABE/portraits.taf

SITE DESCRIPTION. The National Association for Bilingual Education (NABE), the Northeast and Islands Regional Educational Laboratory at Brown University, and Boston College have joined to develop a national database of successful bilingual education programs. Visitors to the site can learn about the selection process, read about model programs, and nominate programs to be considered for listing.

HIGHLIGHTS FOR DISTRICT LEADERS. Curriculum and bilingual education coordinators can find nationwide examples of elementary and middle school programs where limited English proficient students (LEPs) have found academic success.

CURRICULUM AND INSTRUCTION

Association for Supervision and Curriculum Development

www.ascd.org

ORGANIZATION DESCRIPTION. The Association for Supervision and Curriculum Development (ASCD) is an international organization that focuses its attention and resources on issues in staff development and curriculum. Membership is open to educators, school board members, parents, and students.

BENEFITS OF MEMBERSHIP. Several levels of membership offer increasing levels of service. All members receive eight issues of *Educational Leadership* magazine annually, along with two newsletters, discounts on products and conferences, and access to the members-only areas of the Web site. For an additional fee, ASCD also offers membership in affiliate organizations and networks.

SITE DESCRIPTION. The three primary areas of interest for district leaders are:

- **News and Issues:** Briefs, articles, policy updates, and other education news.

- **Education Topics:** Short multimedia lessons on topics such as inclusion and multicultural education.

- **Professional Development:** Information about training opportunities, including conferences, academies, tutorials, videos, online opportunities, and more.

HIGHLIGHTS FOR DISTRICT LEADERS. ASCD offers a number of excellent resources for district leaders. Visit the **News & Issues** area, where you can sign up for a free subscription to the online daily *SmartBrief* e-newsletter, or download the ASCD Advocacy Kit. You can also access online articles here. Check out **Education Topics**, where you can explore various online resources on topics such as curriculum integration, mentoring, problem-based learning, and so on. Explore discussion threads in the **Online Activities** area of **Professional Development.**

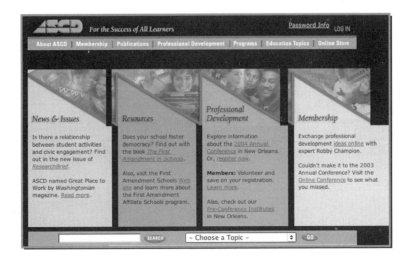

CURRICULUM AND INSTRUCTION

Content Knowledge—3rd Edition

www.mcrel.org/standards-benchmarks

SITE DESCRIPTION. Sponsored by Mid-continent Research for Education and Learning, this easy-to-use site offers a searchable database of national standards in content areas ranging from language arts and mathematics to the arts and behavioral science.

HIGHLIGHTS FOR DISTRICT LEADERS. In addition to the standards database, the **Lesson Plans** link leads to multiple collections of standards-based lesson plans in all major content areas. The fourth editions of language arts, mathematics, and science standards can also be accessed through a link on the Home page.

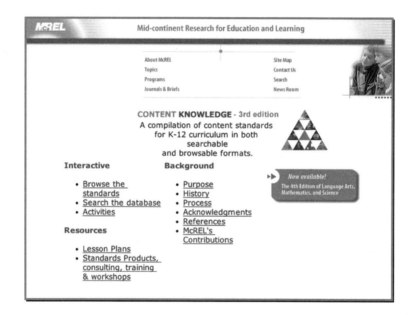

CURRICULUM AND INSTRUCTION

Exploration in Learning and Instruction: The Theory Into Practice Database
http://tip.psychology.org

SITE DESCRIPTION. The purpose of this site is to provide a resource where educators can easily access information about learning and instructional theory. Using a simple database, visitors can find summaries of 50 major theories. The information can also be accessed by learning domain and/or concept.

HIGHLIGHTS FOR DISTRICT LEADERS. It's important for educators and leaders to use common definitions when discussing learning and instructional theories. This site provides brief summaries that can help get everyone on the same page. Each summary provides an overview of the theory, the theory's scope or application, examples of its application, the theory's underlying principles, and references. Use this site in preparation for curriculum discussions with administrators and teachers.

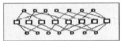

Explorations in Learning & Instruction: The Theory Into Practice Database

Welcome to the Theory Into Practice (TIP) database!

TIP is a tool intended to make learning and instructional theory more accessible to educators. The database contains brief summaries of 50 major theories of learning and instruction. These theories can also be accessed by learning domains and concepts.

- About TIP
- The theories
- Learning domains
- Learning concepts
- About the Author
- Other related web sites

For more information about many of the theories and theorists included here, see the "People & History" section of http://www.psychology.org

Copyright 1994-2003 Greg Kearsley (gkearsley@sprynet.com) http://home.sprynet.com/~gkearsley

CURRICULUM AND INSTRUCTION

Federal Resources for Educational Excellence

www.ed.gov/free

SITE DESCRIPTION. More than 30 federal agencies have joined to offer teaching and learning resources for all major content areas through this "FREE" Web site. The site is updated monthly.

HIGHLIGHTS FOR DISTRICT LEADERS. Site leaders and teachers often look to the district for support materials and resources. Use the content area links as well as the **More for Students** area to identify a wide variety of materials. When visiting the **What is FREE?** area, be sure to click on the **CE Toolkit** link. These downloadable resources can be used to design professional development for teachers who want to learn more about technology integration.

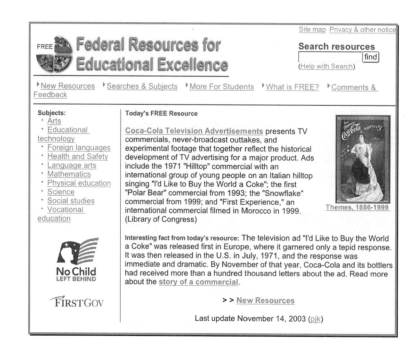

EARLY CHILDHOOD EDUCATION

Everything for Early Childhood Education: EduPuppy

www.edupuppy.com

SITE DESCRIPTION. This site brings together a broad collection of resources and materials for early childhood educators and parents of young children in preschool through Grade 3. The **Search by Category** area offers links to research, articles, information for administrators, early childhood education (ECE) advocacy, activities, and much more.

HIGHLIGHTS FOR DISTRICT LEADERS. There are a number of areas that early childhood specialists will want to explore. At this time, following the **Search by Category** link is the easiest way to see the full spectrum of available resources. Come to this section and click on **Administrators** to access publications and other resources for district ECE specialists. The **ECE Advocacy** link leads to information about laws and regulations as well as relevant sections of the No Child Left Behind legislation. The **Articles** link is organized by content area, as well as professional, technology, and No Child Left Behind headings. The **Research** link takes you to articles about learning theory and early childhood development. Sign up for EduPuppy's free online newsletter.

EARLY CHILDHOOD EDUCATION

National Association for Education of Young Children

www.naeyc.org

ORGANIZATION DESCRIPTION. Founded in 1926, the National Association for Education of Young Children (NAEYC) has more than 100,000 members dedicated to improving education for children from birth through Grade 3.

BENEFITS OF MEMBERSHIP. There are three levels of national membership, as well as membership through a local affiliate. Regular and student members receive six issues of the NAEYC journal *Young Children,* reduced registration rates for conferences and seminars, access to the members-only area of the Web site, and reduced subscription rates for *Early Childhood Research Quarterly.* Comprehensive members receive the benefits of regular and student members as well as five or six NAEYC books each year.

SITE DESCRIPTION. Nonmembers of NAEYC can access important information in the following areas:

- **Public Policy:** Research reports, federal and state policies and legislation, and critical issues.

- **Parents:** Short articles for parents and educators.

HIGHLIGHTS FOR DISTRICT LEADERS. The **Public Policy** area contains valuable information for district leaders on current research and legislation related to early childhood education. You may also want to review the short articles in the **Parents** area to share with site leaders.

EARLY CHILDHOOD EDUCATION

Technology in Early Childhood Education
www.netc.org/earlyconnections

SITE DESCRIPTION. Hosted by the Northwest Regional Educational Laboratory and the Northwest Educational Technology Consortium, this site takes a balanced approach to the benefits and drawbacks of technology use among very young children. The various links explore **Children's Development, Technology Connections, Publications,** and **Common Questions.**

HIGHLIGHTS FOR DISTRICT LEADERS. District leaders making programmatic and purchasing decisions for early childhood programs need to visit the **Children's Development** and **Technology Connections** areas. Each section looks at critical questions for various program settings: child care, preschool, kindergarten, primary grades, and before/after school.

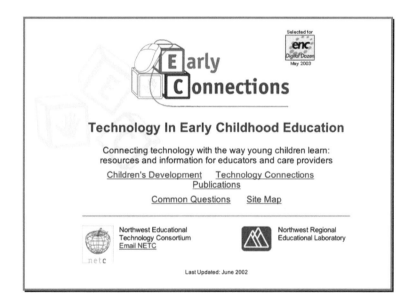

GRANT WRITING

Getting Grants: Finding Funding Sources Online
www.libraryspot.com/features/grantsfeature.html

SITE DESCRIPTION. This page on the LibrarySpot Web site offers numerous links for grant writers who are looking for potential funding sources and/or tips to improve their proposals.

HIGHLIGHTS FOR DISTRICT LEADERS. Given the ever-shifting nature of the educational finance landscape, you may find an occasional dead link here. However, this collection of resources for grant writers is so comprehensive that it's worth visiting on a regular basis. Three areas are particularly useful:

- **Do Your Homework:** Links to sites that offer proposal development resources.

- **Government Sources:** A list of grants currently offered by various governmental agencies.

- **Foundations:** Potential nonprofit funding sources.

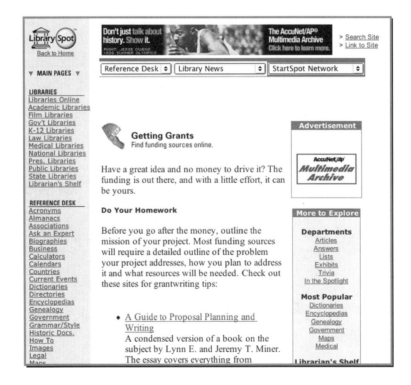

GRANT WRITING

Grantionary

www.eduplace.com/grants/help/grantionary.html

SITE DESCRIPTION. Created and maintained by Houghton Mifflin Company, this is an online glossary of terms related to grant writing.

HIGHLIGHTS FOR DISTRICT LEADERS. If you're new to writing grant proposals, or are working with new grant writers, this handy glossary is very helpful. You might also want to check out the **Grant and Funding** and **Help With Grant Writing** links at the bottom of the page.

Grants & Funding

Grantionary

A Glossary of Terms Related to Grants and Funding

Term or Acronym	Definition	How Used
Grant Seeker	person, school, district, etc. who is applying for the grant	This term is used in workshops, journals, etc.
Grantee	person, school, district, etc. who receives the grant	This term is used in applications and instructions.
Grantor or Grant Maker	agency, organization, etc. who is providing the grant	This term is used in applications and instructions.
RFA	Request for Application	a call for grant applications—a simpler format than RFP
RFP	Request for Proposal	a call for grant proposals – more complex, narrative format

---

GRANT WRITING

Grants and Contracts

www.ed.gov/fund/landng.jhtml

SITE DESCRIPTION. This site offers comprehensive information about federal education grant opportunities. The **Grants, Contracts,** and **Awards, Accounts & Reporting** links include information you can use to find grants, make applications, and follow reporting guidelines.

HIGHLIGHTS FOR DISTRICT LEADERS. In addition to using the links mentioned above, review the **Features** section on the main page. **Features** includes links to documents and online tools that provide important information about grant programs, funding forecasts, and Federal Register notices. You can also subscribe to the free online *EDInfo* newsletter, sent out one or two times each week with updates on grant information.

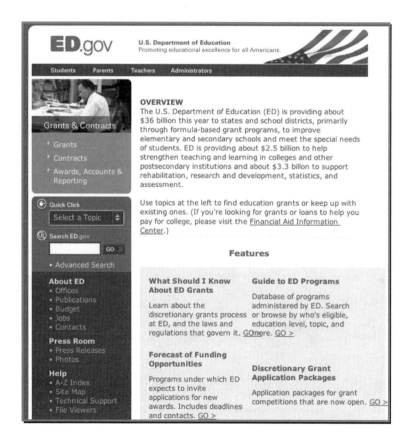

GRANT WRITING

SchoolGrants

www.schoolgrants.org

SITE DESCRIPTION. Established in 1999, this site offers instruction on how to write grants, as well as information about grant-writing opportunities.

HIGHLIGHTS FOR DISTRICT LEADERS. A visit to the **Grant Writing Tips** section leads to basic information that helps grant writers develop successful proposals, hire consultants as grant writers, write letters of inquiry, and evaluate proposals. **Sample Proposals** includes links to actual proposals that can be used as models for your own. **Grant Opportunities** are organized into **Federal, State,** and **Foundation** categories. Check here for ideas about possible funding sources.

For the kids ... www.schoolgrants.org

Welcome to SchoolGrants!
Your one-stop site for PK-12 school grant opportunities

Home

What's New

Services
  Vendors

Newsletters

Let's Write a Grant CD

Bring Home the Bacon
Listserv

Grant Writing
Grant Writing Tips
Grant Opportunities

Sample Proposals

Fundraising
Opportunities

News of Interest

Links/Resources

Note: While you may use any browser you wish, this site is optimized for use with Internet Explorer.

SchoolGrants was created in 1999 as a way to share grant information with PK-12 educators. Grant writing can be intimidating to those who are new at it. SchoolGrants helps ease those fears by providing online tips to those who need them. Finding suitable grant opportunities requires a great deal of time and research - SchoolGrants reduces the effort by listing a variety of opportunities available to public and private nonprofit elementary and secondary schools and districts across the United States.

PUPIL PERSONNEL

The Behavior Home Page

www.state.ky.us/agencies/behave/homepage.html

SITE DESCRIPTION. Developed for Kentucky educators by the Kentucky Department of Education and the Department of Special Education and Rehabilitation Counseling at the University of Kentucky, this site is an excellent resource for any district leader dealing with student behavior issues. General resources include **Interactive Features, Behavior Interventions, Academic Connection, Law,** and links to other online resources.

HIGHLIGHTS FOR DISTRICT LEADERS. Begin with the **Behavior Interventions** area, where you will find support for behavioral issues at three different levels: universal (school-wide), targeted (small groups), and intensive (chronic problems, often with individual students). The **Academic Connection** area focuses on the impact of behavior on student performance, offering articles and links to professional organizations related to this topic. Federal law and regulations are addressed in the **Law** area, and any site visitor may post discipline-related questions in the **Behavior Home Page Discussion Forum** found in the **Interactive Features** area of the Web site.

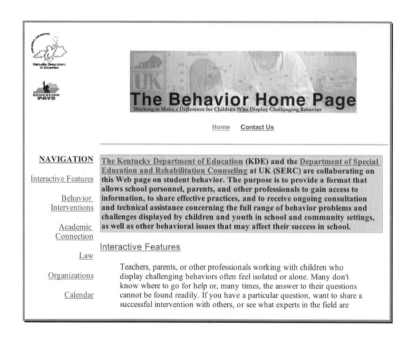

PUPIL PERSONNEL

National School Public Relations Association

www.nspra.org

ORGANIZATION DESCRIPTION. The National School Public Relations Association (NSPRA) has been providing services to schools and districts in the United States and Canada since 1935. Its mission is to build support for education through responsible communication.

BENEFITS OF MEMBERSHIP. There are several levels of organizational and individual membership. Membership benefits vary by membership type but include newsletter subscriptions and discounts on products and seminar fees.

SITE DESCRIPTION. Nonmembers of NSPRA can access useful information in the following areas:

- **Starting a School PR Program:** Documents, tools, and advice about starting a public relations program for your district.

- **School PR Articles:** Short articles on school safety and other public relations issues for district and site leaders.

- **Sample of NSPRA Publications:** Links to articles in past issues of *Network, Principal Communicator,* and *NSPRA Bonus* publications.

HIGHLIGHTS FOR DISTRICT LEADERS. Establishing good public relations is an important task for district officials. A proactive approach is beneficial to everyone concerned, from students and educators to the local community. The **Starting a School PR Program** link offers district leaders useful guidelines for developing a public relations policy, as well as tips for dealing with media, sample policies, and successful models.

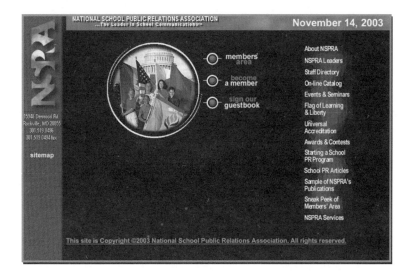

PUPIL PERSONNEL

Office of Safe and Drug-Free Schools
www.ed.gov/about/offices/list/osdfs/

SITE DESCRIPTION. The U.S. Department of Education's Office of Safe and Drug-Free Schools (OSDFS) Web site focuses on administering, coordinating, and recommending policies that reduce violence and drug use on school campuses and promote student health. On this site you will find information about **Programs/Initiatives**, **Reports & Resources**, and **News** about OSDFS initiatives.

HIGHLIGHTS FOR DISTRICT LEADERS. The **Programs/Initiatives** link provides overviews of current programs. To get more specific information about a particular program (such as eligibility requirements or application forms), click on the links within the overview. The **Reports & Resources** link leads to an area where you can access downloadable reports, order free publications, and visit online resources dealing with safety issues.

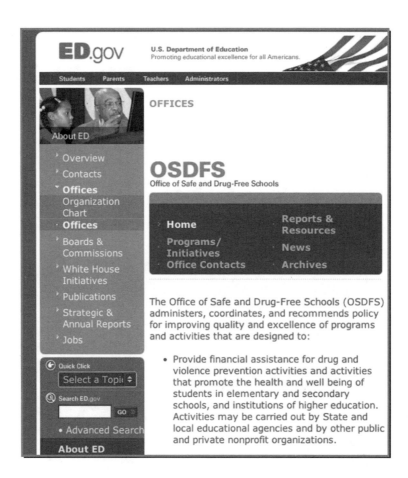

PUPIL PERSONNEL

The SafetyZone

www.safetyzone.org

SITE DESCRIPTION. The Northwest Regional Educational Laboratory sponsors this clearinghouse for information and materials related to school safety issues. Materials are organized in three areas: **Library, Requests,** and **Links. Popular Topics** are also highlighted on the home page.

HIGHLIGHTS FOR DISTRICT LEADERS. Any individual in the United States may browse the **Library** and check out books and videos for a one-month time period. To order free school safety publications you may keep, click on the **Requests** link. The **Links** area allows you to access school safety Web sites and state resources.

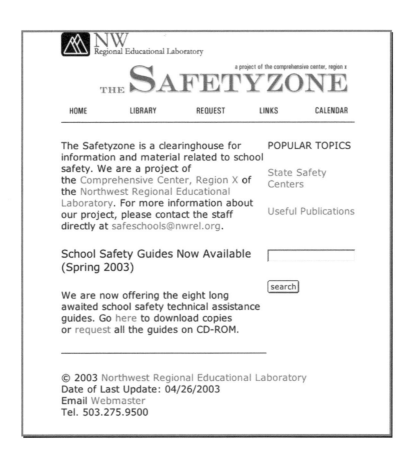

PUPIL PERSONNEL

School Safety

www.nea.org/issues/safescho

SITE DESCRIPTION. The National Education Association (NEA) offers a well-organized school safety section on the organization's Web site. After reading the overview, use the tabs across the top of the page to find **Research**, **NEA Resources**, and **Other Resources** about school safety.

HIGHLIGHTS FOR DISTRICT LEADERS. The **NEA Resources** link offers well-balanced and practical approaches to school safety. Visit this area to see NEA's **School Safety Facts**, good for use with site staff and parents. Be sure to review the **Crisis Communications Guide and Toolkit,** which provides practical information for district leaders creating or updating a school safety plan.

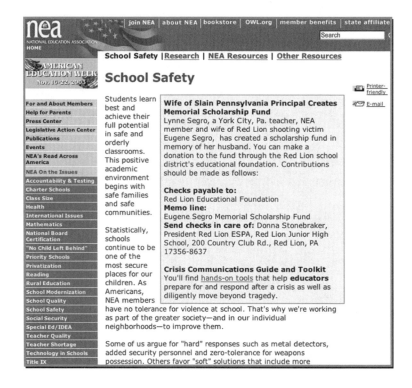

SPECIAL EDUCATION

Center for Applied Special Technology

www.cast.org

SITE DESCRIPTION. The Center for Applied Special Technology (CAST) is a nonprofit organization whose mission is to explore ways that technology can be used to expand learning opportunities for people with disabilities. The Web site is organized into four areas:

- **About CAST:** The mission and vision of CAST, as well as the people and organizations that support it.

- **Universal Design for Learning:** Theory, research, tools, examples, and activities that address the needs of individual learners.

- **National Center on Accessing the General Curriculum:** Information about making the general curriculum accessible to students with special needs.

- **CAST Products:** Free and low-cost materials that support individualized needs and resolve access issues.

HIGHLIGHTS FOR DISTRICT LEADERS. Both the **Universal Design for Learning** and the **National Center on Accessing the General Curriculum** areas are filled with up-to-date information for district leaders who are dealing with issues of individualized learning and universal student access to the curriculum. Once you've reviewed either of these areas, visit the **CAST Products** section, where you can access an online version of the book *Learning to Read in the Computer Age*. You can also learn more about *Bobby,* a free tool educators can use to check how well students with special needs are able to access pages on the school's Web site. The tool also suggests how to repair identified barriers to access.

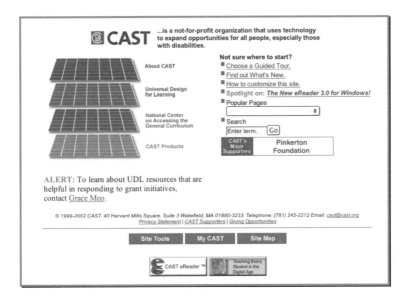

SPECIAL EDUCATION

Council for Exceptional Children

www.cec.sped.org

ORGANIZATION DESCRIPTION. The Council for Exceptional Children (CEC) is an international organization seeking opportunities for students who are gifted or have exceptional learning needs or disabilities.

BENEFITS OF MEMBERSHIP. Professional and student memberships include subscriptions to two journals *(TEACHING Exceptional Children and Exceptional Children)* and one newsletter *(CEC Today)*, as well as discounts for conferences and CEC publications and products. Associate memberships for parents include everything but the subscription to *Exceptional Children.* Premier members receive all of the above plus policy information, the president's quarterly update, and conference privileges.

SITE DESCRIPTION. The home page highlights CEC-related activities. Links lead to information useful to members and nonmembers alike, including:

- **Public Policy & Advocacy/Legislative Action Center:** Information about current legislation and e-mail links to Congress members.

- **CEC Discussion Forums:** Online discussions for educators.

- **Yes I Can! Foundation for Exceptional Children:** Opportunities for educators and students; information on student scholarships and mini-grants for teachers.

- **IDEA Partnerships:** Four national projects focused on implementation of IDEA.

- **ERIC Clearinghouse on Disabilities and Gifted Education:** A national source for articles and other materials related to special needs and gifted education.

HIGHLIGHTS FOR DISTRICT LEADERS. The **Public Policy & Advocacy** and **IDEA Partnership** links are excellent resources for legal issues related to special and gifted education.

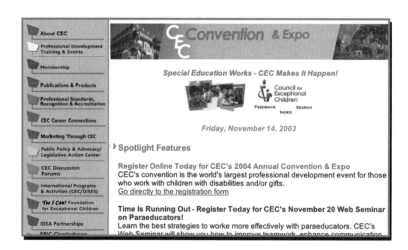

SPECIAL EDUCATION

National Center for Learning Disabilities
www.ncld.org

SITE DESCRIPTION. This Web site is a resource for educators and parents who are seeking information about learning disabilities. Three primary areas are of interest to educators:

- **LD InfoZone:** Resources, fact sheets, and research news.
- **Living with LD:** Information for teens and adults with learning disabilities.
- **LD Advocate:** Public policy in action and public policy initiatives.

HIGHLIGHTS FOR DISTRICT LEADERS. In the **LD InfoZone**, use the **Resource Locator** to find links to resources specific to your state, or download Fact Sheets about various learning disabilities. **Research News** provides access to several downloadable studies on learning disabilities. Go to the **LD Advocate** area to review national statistics about students with learning disabilities, to download state-by-state profiles of learning disabilities, or to read about national initiatives.

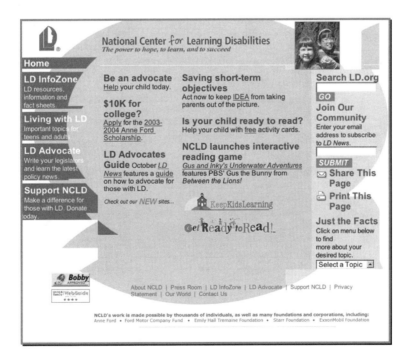

SPECIAL EDUCATION

SchwabLearning.org

www.schwablearning.org

SITE DESCRIPTION. SchwabLearning is a program sponsored by the Charles and Helen Schwab Foundation. The Web site is designed to provide support to parents of children with learning disabilities. There is a companion Web site designed for the children themselves. Educators may request permission to reprint Schwab articles posted on the site so that they can be shared with parents.

HIGHLIGHTS FOR DISTRICT LEADERS. Use the tabs across the top of the home page to view articles that take parents through the process of **Identifying** and **Managing** disabilities. Visit the **Resources** area to find downloadable booklets about learning disabilities and an informative online newsletter. Schwab also sponsors a site for children ages 8–12 who have learning disabilities. It can be accessed through the home page, or by going directly to **www.schwablearning.org/SparkTop/.**

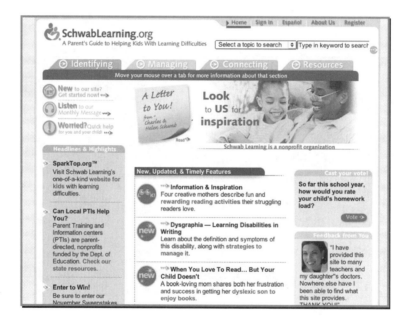

SPECIAL PROJECTS

Especially for Parents

www.ed.gov/parents/landing/jhtml?src=pn

SITE DESCRIPTION. The U.S. Department of Education offers several publications that educators may download and share with parents. Topics range from preparing children to attend school for the first time all the way to finding the right college. Topic areas listed on the left side of the page contain multiple resources. There are also featured items listed on the main page.

HIGHLIGHTS FOR DISTRICT LEADERS. This site provides a wealth of material that can be used for parent workshops, meetings, and teacher conferences. Find the topics that relate to current initiatives in your district and explore the multitude of available resources.

SPECIAL PROJECTS

National PTA

www.pta.org

SITE DESCRIPTION. Parent outreach often falls under the auspices of the special projects department of the district office. The National PTA Web site offers information district leaders can use to increase parental involvement in their children's education.

HIGHLIGHTS FOR DISTRICT LEADERS. Visit the **Parent Involvement** section of the site to find useful parent education materials addressing topics such as **Help Your Child Succeed, Health & Safety**, and **Drugs & Alcohol**. The **PTA and Washington** link includes Action Alerts and Legislative Information helpful to both parents and district leaders.

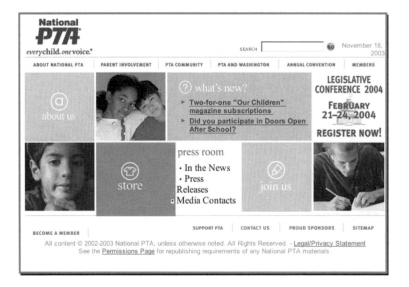

SPECIAL PROJECTS

No Child Left Behind

www.ed.gov/nclb/landing.jhtml

SITE DESCRIPTION. The No Child Left Behind Act (NCLB), signed into law in January 2002, largely revamped the Elementary and Secondary Education Act (ESEA). The U.S. Department of Education's NCLB Web site provides an overview of the legislation, as well as in-depth explanations of the four guiding principles of NCLB: stronger accountability, more local freedom, proven methods, and choices for parents.

HIGHLIGHTS FOR DISTRICT LEADERS. Click on the **Administrators** link at the top of the page to access documents such as *Guidance on No Child Left Behind (NCLB)* and *Accountability: Questions and Answers.* Several additional links on this page lead to resources for administrators implementing NCLB, including **Lead and Manage My School, Strengthen Teacher Quality, Work with Parents & the Community,** and **Find Grants.**

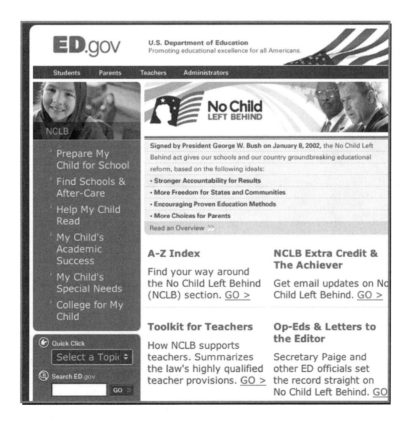

SPECIAL PROJECTS

Office of Vocational and Adult Education

www.ed.gov/about/offices/list/ovae

SITE DESCRIPTION. The U.S. Department of Education's Office of Vocational and Adult Education (OVAE) focuses on postsecondary education for teens and adults, providing resources and research on best practices. Links of interest include:

- **Programs/Initiatives:** Grants and programs available through OVAE.

- **Reports & Resources:** Research reports and data, links to related information, and state resources.

- **High Schools:** Links include **Facts and Figures** and **Topics in High School Education.**

- **Career and Technical Education:** Information about Vocational Education.

- **Adult Education and Literacy:** Important information for educators planning programs that meet requirements of No Child Left Behind.

HIGHLIGHTS FOR DISTRICT LEADERS. While most information here is for high school level district leaders, the **Adult Education and Literacy** link is pertinent for K–12 leaders who are writing plans that must be NCLB-compliant. Use the **Reports & Resources** link to access Facts at a Glance for high schools, community colleges, and adult education programs.

SPECIAL PROJECTS

Regional Educational Laboratories Network

www.relnetwork.org

SITE DESCRIPTION. The Regional Educational Laboratories (REL) Network consists of 10 regional laboratories located around the country. Supported by the U.S. Department of Education, Institute of Education Sciences, the labs work with educators in their regions on issues of school reform and improvement. In addition, each lab takes the lead nationally in one or more leadership areas. The labs offer low- and no-cost resources through their online network.

HIGHLIGHTS FOR DISTRICT LEADERS. Use the **National Leadership Areas** link to find the lab that specializes in your interest area. For example, "resources for family" and "community connections to schools" will be found on the Southwest Educational Development Laboratory's Web site. Resources for educators working with diverse learners are housed on the Education Alliance at Brown University Web site. Take the time to visit your own region's lab online to learn more about the services and products available to your district.

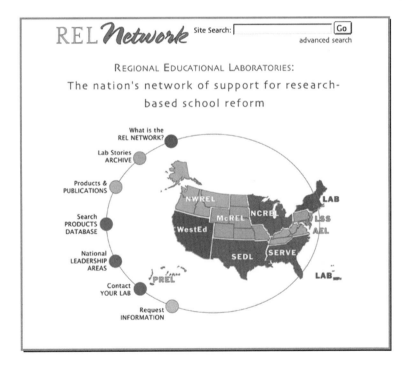

SPECIAL PROJECTS

Student Achievement and School Accountability Programs
www.ed.gov/about/offices/list/oese/sasa

SITE DESCRIPTION. The Student Achievement and School Accountability Office of the U.S. Department of Education supports efforts to improve student academic achievement in low-income community schools, primarily through Title I programs.

HIGHLIGHTS FOR DISTRICT LEADERS. The **Programs/Initiatives** link leads to a list of all programs overseen by this office. Click on a program title for a description. The **Reports & Resources** link takes you to a page where you can access reports and articles related to Title I programs. The **Standards/Accountability** area includes information about adequate yearly progress, assessment instruments, state accountability plans, and more.

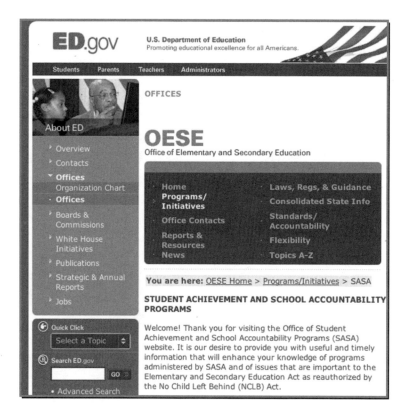

TECHNOLOGY

Center for Applied Research in Educational Technology

http://caret.iste.org

SITE DESCRIPTION. The International Society for Technology in Education (ISTE) is working in partnership with Educational Support Systems in San Mateo, California, to develop a searchable database of research studies and other information about technology use in education. The Sacramento County Office of Education created the site, called the Center for Applied Research in Educational Technology (CARET). The effort is funded by the Bill and Melinda Gates Foundation.

HIGHLIGHTS FOR DISTRICT LEADERS. You can access the information in several ways. By clicking on **Browse Questions & Answers**, you will find links to research focused on student learning, curriculum and instruction, online teaching and learning, professional development, and assessment and evaluation. Click on the topic area of interest, and you find a list of hyperlinked questions. By clicking on a question, you are taken directly to information answering the question. For example, learn more about how teacher technology standards can be met by clicking on **Professional Development,** and then clicking on the question about teacher technology standards. You can also access information by using the search option, which returns results based upon keywords you enter or study characteristics you select. The CARET **Glossary** defines statistical and technical terms.

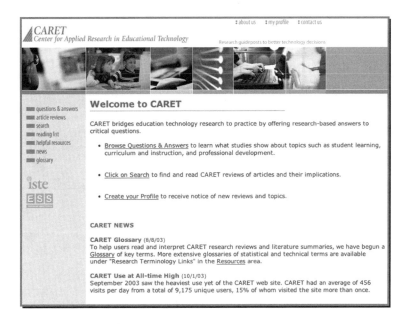

TECHNOLOGY

eSchoolNews Online

www.eschoolnews.com

SITE DESCRIPTION. eSchool News Online features articles about technology in education, as well as a number of resources for educators, including:

- **School Technology Buyer's Guide:** Online information about vendors, products, and services for K–12 educators.

- **Forums:** Current discussion areas, including No Child Left Behind (NCLB), Worst Practices in School Technology, and Significant Issues & Emerging Trends.

- **eNewsletters:** Two free weekly e-newsletters.

- **Funding Center:** Funding news and information about grant opportunities.

- **Special Reports:** Summaries of important technology issues.

HIGHLIGHTS FOR DISTRICT LEADERS. Access to some areas requires free registration. Visit the **eNewsletters** section to sign up for *eSchool News This Week* and *Tools for Schools,* two excellent sources of technology news for busy district leaders. All summaries in these e-newsletters link back to the eSchool News site for complete information. The **Funding Center** articles are very helpful, as are the **Special Reports** on topics such as tablet computing, handheld computing, and data management for NCLB success.

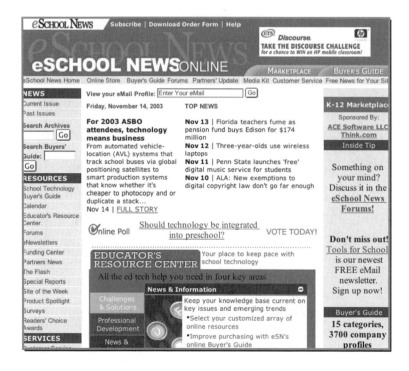

TECHNOLOGY

International Society for Technology in Education

www.iste.org

ORGANIZATION DESCRIPTION. The International Society for Technology in Education (ISTE) is a nonprofit professional membership organization representing instructional technology leaders around the world. ISTE promotes appropriate use of technology to support teaching and learning, as well as school administration.

BENEFITS OF MEMBERSHIP. A subscription to *ISTE Update* newsletter and either *Learning & Leading with Technology* or the *Journal of Research on Technology in Education*; 10% discount on books published by ISTE; conferences, workshops, and other professional development opportunities; national advocacy activities.

SITE DESCRIPTION. There are five areas of particular interest for district leaders:

- **Publications:** Link to current and back issues of *Learning & Leading with Technology (L&L)*. Download articles or read them online.

- **NETS:** The National Educational Technology Standards, developed for students, teachers, and administrators, including numerous links to support materials.

- **Professional Development:** Conferences, workshops, and symposia.

- **Educator Resources:** Books, Web sites, and periodicals on technology in education.

- **Research Projects:** White papers, studies, and reports.

HIGHLIGHTS FOR DISTRICT LEADERS. Visit the **NETS** area to access information about technology standards for students, teachers, and administrators. This extensive resource includes standards, performance indicators, and support material such as profiles and lesson plans. For supporting documentation, visit the **Research Projects** area, particularly the **Center for Applied Research in Educational Technology (CARET)** and the **Reports** section.

TECHNOLOGY

Network of Regional Technology in Education Consortia
www.rtec.org

SITE DESCRIPTION. Funded by the U.S. Department of Education, the 10 national Regional Technology in Education Consortia (R*TEC) Centers serve regions aligned with the 10 national Regional Education Laboratories. The purpose of these centers is to assist educators in effectively using advanced technologies in the classroom. You can access any of the individual centers from this page and also find highlights of products and resources available from all centers.

HIGHLIGHTS FOR DISTRICT LEADERS. Visit the **R*TEC Resources and Products** area to get a quick overview of materials available through the various centers. You'll find publications, surveys, technology planning and training materials, and more. The **Education Technology News** area is great for getting a quick update on hot topics in educational technology.

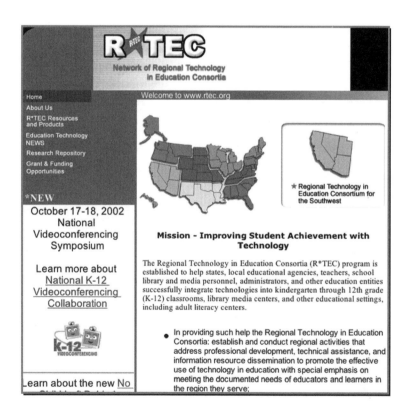

TECHNOLOGY

Planning for Technology: Putting the Pieces Together
www.edgateway.net/cs/tk/print/rtec_docs/tk_home.html

SITE DESCRIPTION. This nine-part tool kit is designed for use by district leaders as they develop and implement student-centered technology integration plans. Topics include district-level planning, integration, professional development, assessment and evaluation, and more.

HIGHLIGHTS FOR DISTRICT LEADERS. The site employs the metaphor of a jigsaw puzzle, with each piece of technology planning being an integral part of the whole. You access each area by clicking on its puzzle piece. Begin with the **Tech Planning Tool Kit Overview** to orient yourself to the site. From there, choose the puzzle piece topics most relevant to your current needs. Be sure to visit the **Integrating Technology with Standards** and the **Technology Enhanced Instructional Units** areas, which include links to samples of technology-infused lessons and units that are also standards-based. The **Technology Skills Assessment: Standards and Rubrics** is also a popular area.

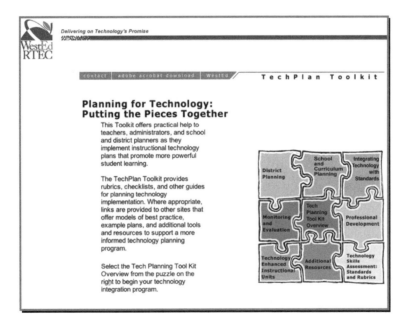

TECHNOLOGY

Technology Briefs for NCLB Planners
www.neirtec.org/products/techbriefs/

SITE DESCRIPTION. The No Child Left Behind (NCLB) Act emphasizes the use of technology throughout various instructional programs designed to increase student performance. The Technology Briefs available here are designed to assist district leaders in planning programs that reflect appropriate technology use. They are also useful in applying for federal funding that falls under NCLB.

HIGHLIGHTS FOR DISTRICT LEADERS. You will want to download each Technology Brief as a reference during the planning and application process. Briefs include suggested strategies, questions to consider during the planning process, and resources. The briefs are free, but you will be asked to fill out a short survey before you can download the files.

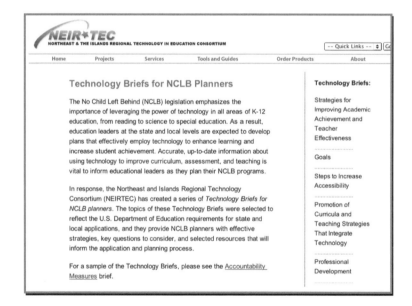

TECHNOLOGY

Technology Information Center for Administrative Leadership

www.portical.org

SITE DESCRIPTION. The Technology Information Center for Administrative Leadership (TICAL) site is a special project funded by the California Department of Education. It targets school administrators and their technology needs. Hundreds of resources reviewed by experienced educators are available. These include:

- **Features: Expert Opinion** articles and narrated PowerPoint presentations on such topics as data-driven decision making, curriculum integration, financial planning, operations and maintenance, professional development, and technology planning.

- **Resource Database:** The heart of this site, with point and click tables for searching specific resources related to district-wide technology implementation.

- **Tools & Templates:** Ready-to-use productivity tools you can download and access.

HIGHLIGHTS FOR DISTRICT LEADERS. The articles and narrated PowerPoint presentations in **Features** are useful springboards for discussion in staff and parent meetings. The **Tools & Templates** area includes many useful items. If you are evaluating an instructional program, for example, download the Analysis of Process template found in **Data-Driven Decision Making**. Visit **Technology Planning** to find templates suitable for use in planning committee meetings. The matrices posted in **Resources** take the guesswork out of finding online resources geared to your technology needs: just specify the topic you're interested in and the type of resource you're looking for. One matrix page is aligned to the National Educational Technology Standards for Administrators (NETS·A).

TESTING, ASSESSMENT, AND RESEARCH

Brown Center on Educational Policy

www.brookings.edu/browncenter

SITE DESCRIPTION. The Brookings Institution is a nonpartisan organization that conducts research and analyzes public policy. This URL takes you directly to the Brown Center on Education Policy, a Brookings affiliate. This site is an excellent resource for research reports, analyses, and commentary regarding American education.

HIGHLIGHTS FOR DISTRICT LEADERS. The full text of reports and articles (analysis and commentary) is available for downloading. Books may also be purchased from this site. The Brown Center's annual reports on education use standardized test scores and surveys to examine student achievement nationally. Download recent reports for your own information and use in making data-driven decisions about instructional programs.

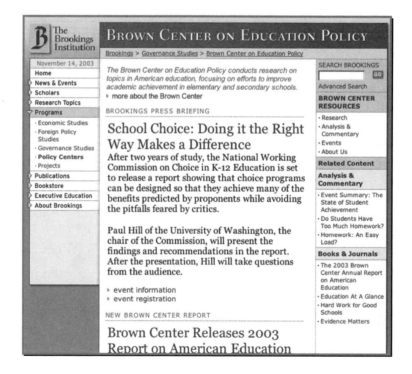

TESTING, ASSESSMENT, AND RESEARCH

National Assessment Governing Board

www.nagb.org

SITE DESCRIPTION. The National Assessment Governing Board (NAGB) consists of 26 members representing educators, state governors and legislators, business representatives, and the general public. The purpose of NAGB is to set policy for the National Assessment of Educational Progress (NAEP), which samples student achievement in several content areas in Grades 4, 8, and 12. This site provides information about policies and results for NAEP.

HIGHLIGHTS FOR DISTRICT LEADERS. Scroll through the home page to find links to recent information about student testing and achievement, including publications, assessment schedules, and news items. Click on the **Publications** link to find a complete listing of NAGB and NAEP frameworks and reports. These materials are free and may be downloaded and printed, or you may order them using online form.

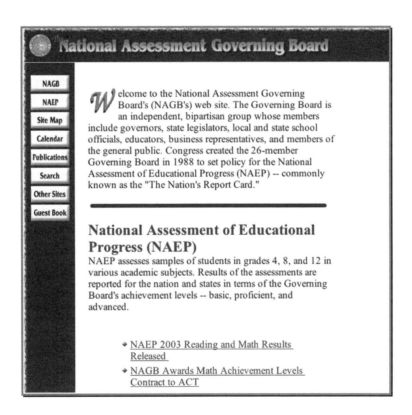

TESTING, ASSESSMENT, AND RESEARCH

National Center for Educational Statistics
http://nces.ed.gov/practitioners/administrators.asp

SITE DESCRIPTION. The National Center for Education Statistics (NCES) provides reports of statistical information about K–12 education in the United States. The site also offers tools that administrators can use to facilitate accessing and using the data. This link takes you directly to the area of the Web site designed for school administrators, but you can also view other sections by clicking on the links for **Teachers, Policymakers, Parents,** and **Librarians.**

HIGHLIGHTS FOR DISTRICT LEADERS. This page has five main areas. **Main Attraction** highlights such important issues for administrators as professional development and infrastructure needs. **Research Department** provides links to reports and statistics. **Administrator Tools** offers links to specific tools and resources for administrators. **General Resources** features past NCES publications, fast facts, and quick tables and figures. **Worth a Click** provides links to useful information outside the NCES Web site.

TESTING, ASSESSMENT, AND RESEARCH

National Center for Research on Evaluation, Standards, and Student Testing

www.cse.ucla.edu

SITE DESCRIPTION. The National Center for Research on Evaluation, Standards, and Student Testing (CRESST) focuses on the assessment of education programs, the design of assessments, and the validity of inferences drawn through assessment. Areas of interest for district leaders are:

- **Newsletters:** Articles about current assessment and accountability issues.

- **Policy Briefs:** Guidance for administrators and policy makers regarding assessment and accountability issues.

- **Inside CRESST:** Access to **Quality School Portfolio.**

- **Ask the Expert:** A place to read and post questions about assessment.

HIGHLIGHTS FOR DISTRICT LEADERS. Check out the **Quality School Portfolio (QSP)**, a free Web-based tool available to schools and districts and designed to assist them in collecting and analyzing student data. **Policy Briefs** are especially helpful for districts working to meet the requirements of No Child Left Behind.

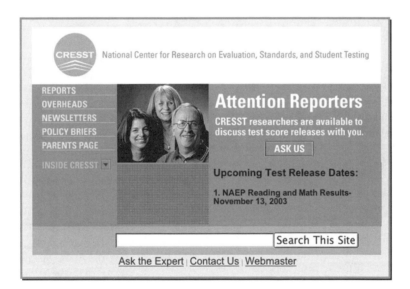

TESTING, ASSESSMENT, AND RESEARCH

Rand Education

www.rand.org/education/

SITE DESCRIPTION. The Rand Corporation "think tank" tackles a wide variety of concerns. This link takes you to Rand's education area. The three areas of emphasis here are assessment and accountability, evaluation of school reform, and teachers and teaching.

HIGHLIGHTS FOR DISTRICT LEADERS. Every current Rand publication is available here. You may purchase bound copies or download and print the files for free. Much of what will likely interest district leaders can be found right on the home page, listed under **New Research** and **New Publications**. You can also download past reports through the **Publications** link.

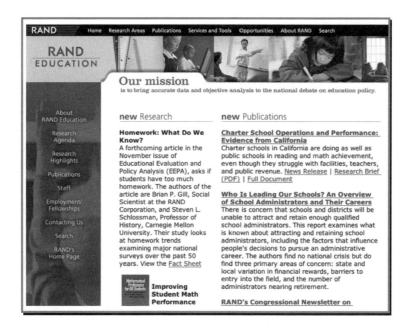

General

The sites included in this section are resources that every district leader will have occasion to use at one time or another. They include publications, organizations, and agencies that address the concerns of every division or department within a district office.

NAME OF SITE/INTERNET ADDRESS	PRIMARY AREA OF EMPHASIS			
	PROFESSIONAL ORGANIZATION	POLICY & LEGISLATION	PLANNING & ACTION	ONLINE JOURNAL
Education Commission of the States www.ecs.org			▓	
Education Week on the Web www.edweek.org				▓
Fed World www.fedworld.gov		▓	▓	
SmartBrief www.smartbrief.com/ascd				▓
U.S. Department of Education www.ed.gov		▓	▓	

Education Commission of the States

www.ecs.org

SITE DESCRIPTION. Since 1965, the Education Commission of the States has worked to improve American education by sharing ideas and information and making policy recommendations. This nonprofit, nonpartisan group of key education leaders, legislators, and businesspeople represents 49 states, the District of Columbia, and three U.S. territories. The commission explores issues in three major areas: **Early Learning, K–12,** and **Postsecondary.**

HIGHLIGHTS FOR DISTRICT LEADERS. Click on the **States & Territories** link to access summaries of the "state of the state" addresses given by each state's governor and the addresses' implications for education. The full text of each address is also available. Access information on current K–12 issues by using either the **Projects & Centers** or the **K–12** link. The lengthy list of issues covered currently includes topics such as **Accountability, Adult Literacy, Assessment, Curriculum, Finance,** and **Teaching Quality.** Each issue is discussed at length, and supporting documentation is also available.

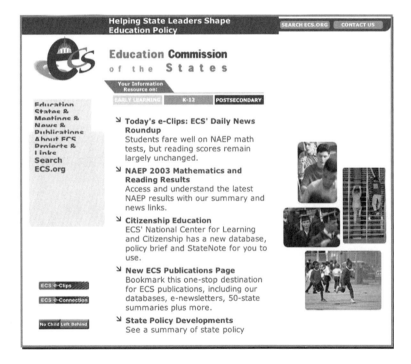

Education Week on the Web

www.edweek.org

SITE DESCRIPTION. In its print version, *Education Week* has been a reliable source of information about education issues for more than 20 years. *Education Week on the Web* offers news, the annual *Quality Counts* and *Technology Counts* reports, and free e-newsletters to help educators stay on top of critical issues.

HIGHLIGHTS FOR DISTRICT LEADERS. Accessing full articles, reports, and newsletters requires free online registration. Two e-newsletters are of particular interest to district leaders: *Teacher Recruiter* (monthly) and *EdWeek Update* (weekly). Each newsletter highlights relevant online articles and provides links to them. **The Daily News** includes links to education articles from national and international newspapers, journals, and magazines. As its title implies, this area is updated every day. Use the **Archives** to search for past articles and special reports. **Top Jobs** will be of interest to district leaders looking for a change.

Fed World

www.fedworld.gov

SITE DESCRIPTION. The Fed World site is designed to make it easy to access information from a variety of governmental agencies, many of which offer education programs.

HIGHLIGHTS FOR DISTRICT LEADERS. The easiest way to find education-related materials is to use the **Top Government Web Sites** link. This area currently provides five ways to find information. You can find government portals and gateways that lead to education information, such as **Computers for Learning or Education–Help for Education,** by clicking and scrolling through the list of choices under **Subject-Based U.S. Government Sites.** The **Federal Register** (which includes information about grant opportunities, executive orders, and so on.) can be accessed through the **Other Important Government Information** drop-down menu. **More Government Sites Links** leads to education-friendly agencies and commissions, such as the **National Endowment for the Humanities** or the **National Science Foundation.**

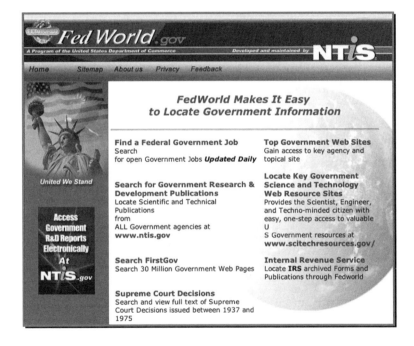

SmartBrief

www.smartbrief.com/ascd

SITE DESCRIPTION. This free e-newsletter is delivered to your e-mail in-box Monday through Friday. Articles dealing with curriculum, professional development, technology solutions, educational policy, association news, and stories from the field are summarized, with links to the full text provided. These articles are culled from various national publications.

HIGHLIGHTS FOR DISTRICT LEADERS. Simply skimming the SmartBrief every day keeps you up to speed on education headlines. When an article catches your eye, click on the link to read the full text. This is one of the best tools for staying on top of trends and issues in education.

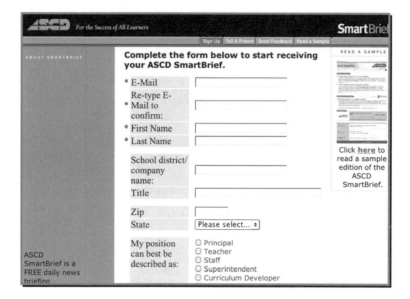

U.S. Department of Education

www.ed.gov

SITE DESCRIPTION. The recently revamped U.S. Department of Education Web site is easier to navigate than in the past. Changes continue to be made that should make the site even more user-friendly. Information about federal education initiatives is now available in five areas:

- **Grants & Contracts**
- **Financial Aid**
- **Research & Statistics**
- **Policy**
- **Programs**

There is also a tab called **Administrators**, which leads to an area for site- and district-level leaders.

HIGHLIGHTS FOR DISTRICT LEADERS. In addition to the self-explanatory links listed above, there are two other features district leaders will want to check out. Click on the **ED newsletters** link to sign up for one or more of the e-newsletters currently available. Ranging from weekly to quarterly, these newsletters offer current information about programs and funding. Use the **Publications** link to access a huge library of free publications appropriate for your own use or to share with staff and parents. The publications can be ordered in print form or downloaded from the site.

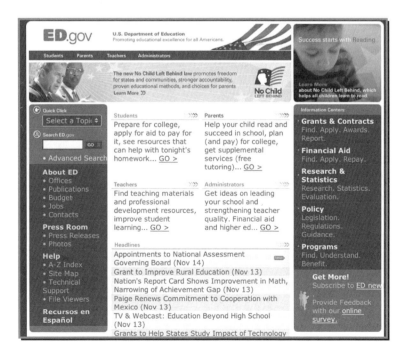

Personal Productivity

There's a fine line between learning a technology well enough to use it on a daily basis to streamline your workload and slipping into doing tasks that should be completed by a clerk or office assistant. The sites listed in this section are included because they can enhance your technological efficiency rather than make you the office guru for any specific hardware or software. You will find tutorials here for using Microsoft Office and other applications, as well as a software program that enables you to download and read PDF files. There are also three Web-based tools: the first allows you to store a list of your bookmarked sites for access from any online computer, the second can be used to create a simple Web site, and the third enables you to create and tabulate online surveys.

NAME OF SITE/INTERNET ADDRESS	PRIMARY AREA OF EMPHASIS			
	INTERNET UTILITIES	SOFTWARE APPLICATIONS	FILE MANAGEMENT	BOOKMARK MANAGEMENT
Add-A-Form www.addaform.com	Online survey creation			
Adobe Acrobat Reader www.adobe.com/products/acrobat/ readstep2.html			Software downloads	
Backflip www.backflip.com				Internet-based management
Education Online for Computer Software www.educationonlineforcomputers.com		Tutorials for applications		
Tripod www.tripod.lycos.com	Web page creation			

Add-A-Form

www.addaform.com

SITE DESCRIPTION. Add-A-Form is a free online service that allows you to create surveys, questionnaires, tests, quizzes, and other online forms to add to a Web site. The basic version allows you to create three forms, which will be hosted for one month each, and tally responses from up to 1,000 respondents. The professional version increases this to 10 forms and 10,000 respondents.

HIGHLIGHTS FOR DISTRICT LEADERS. Online surveys are a quick way to gather data. Think about all the staff surveys you need to conduct each year. These can all be conducted online, saving data entry time and printing costs. Results are presented in a summary format. The professional version also allows you to download raw data in FileMaker, Access, or Excel formats.

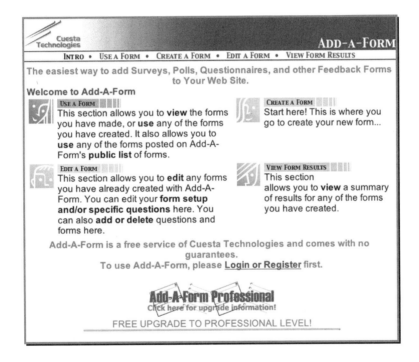

Adobe Acrobat Reader

www.adobe.com/products/acrobat/readstep2.html

SITE DESCRIPTION. From this page you can download and install a free copy of Adobe Acrobat Reader. This software enables you to download, read, and print files that are in Portable Document Format (PDF).

HIGHLIGHTS FOR DISTRICT LEADERS. These days it's very common to find documents that are accessible and downloadable from the Web in PDF format. To access and use the files, you simply need to download a free copy of Adobe Acrobat Reader. Sites that offer PDF documents often include a direct link to the Adobe download page. In that case, click on the link (often an Adobe icon) and follow the download directions. You can also go directly to the Adobe site to download the program. Once it's installed, you're all set to go when you encounter PDF files on the Web.

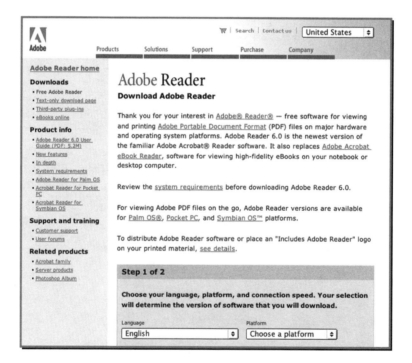

Backflip

www.backflip.com

SITE DESCRIPTION. Backflip is a free Web-based service where you can bookmark and organize Web sites you'd like to visit again. You register for an account, and then follow the simple directions to get started.

HIGHLIGHTS FOR DISTRICT LEADERS. Have you had the experience of finding a site you really like only to try to return later and not be able to find it? Or have you bookmarked a site at the office and then not been able to access it from home? If you use just one computer system, the bookmarks in your browser are sufficient once you know how to use them. But if you use more than one computer (such as at the office and at home), browser-based bookmarks are limited because they are stored only on the system you are using when you set up the bookmark. Backflip, however, is Web-based. When you bookmark a site using your Backflip account, you can access it later from any Internet-connected computer system by logging on to your account. You can also create a list (or folder) of sites and e-mail it to colleagues.

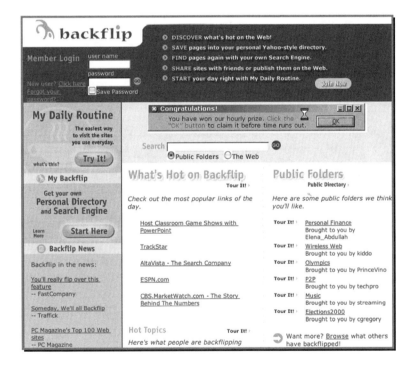

Education Online for Computer Software
www.educationonlineforcomputers.com

SITE DESCRIPTION. This site offers free and fee-based tutorials for users who want to learn how to use various computer applications, including Microsoft programs such as Word, Excel, Access, PowerPoint, Outlook, and FrontPage. Tutorials are also available for programs such as Dreamweaver and Photoshop. The list of free tutorials is extensive and covers beginning, intermediate, and advanced levels of use.

HIGHLIGHTS FOR DISTRICT LEADERS. If you want to learn more about using a word processor, spreadsheet, database, or other application for your own productivity, take a look at this site. The tutorials are self-paced and include tips and tricks for making better use of the software. This is also a great resource to share with staff.

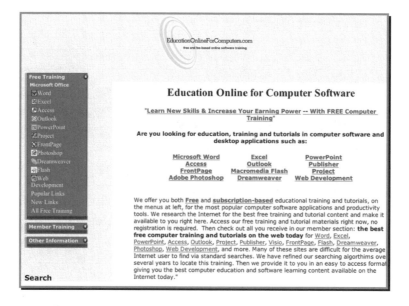

Tripod

www.tripod.lycos.com

SITE DESCRIPTION. Tripod allows users to build their own Web sites using a variety of templates that require no programming experience. You can even post your Web site for free, though this option requires your site to carry a number of ads (over which you have little control). For $4.95 per month, however, your site can be ad-free.

HIGHLIGHTS FOR DISTRICT LEADERS. You may want to set up a Web site for your department for a special project or program. Tripod offers an easy-to-use solution for this kind of special circumstance. In addition to setting up pages, you can link to outside Internet resources and upload text and graphics files that can then be accessed through links you create on a page. Paid subscribers to Tripod may also build a free Weblog or "Blog," a type of Web site that is often used as an online journal. Blogs can be useful for committee work and ongoing discussions.

Personnel

This section of the directory focuses on three areas vital to the work of the personnel department:

- **Human Resources:** Featured sites provide information about a professional organization, employee/employer rights, and employment statistics.

- **Professional Development:** These sites focus on design principles for professional development.

- **Teacher Quality:** Sites here cover preservice and inservice training, professional teaching standards, and teacher evaluation.

QUICK REFERENCE CHART

NAME OF SITE/INTERNET ADDRESS	PRIMARY AREA OF EMPHASIS			
	PROFESSIONAL ORGANIZATION	POLICY & LEGISLATION	PLANNING & ACTION	ONLINE JOURNAL
HUMAN RESOURCES:				
American Association of School Personnel Administrators (AASPA) www.aaspa.com	■			
Electronic Privacy Information Center (EPIC) www.epic.org		■		
Social Security Online www.ssa.gov		■		
U.S. Department of Labor: Bureau of Labor Statistics (BLS) www.bls.gov		■	■	
U.S. Equal Employment Opportunity Commission (EEOC) www.eeoc.gov		■		
PROFESSIONAL DEVELOPMENT:				
e-Lead: Leadership for Student Learning www.e-lead.org			■	
National Staff Development Council (NSDC) www.nsdc.org	■			
TEACHER QUALITY:				
ERIC Clearinghouse on Teaching and Teacher Education www.ericsp.org/pages/about/index.html			■	
National Board for Professional Teaching Standards (NBPTS) www.nbpts.org		■		
National Governors Association: Teacher Quality www.nga.org/center/topics/ 1,1188,D_401,00.html			■	
Teacher Evaluation: New Directions and Practices www.teacherevaluation.net			■	
Teacher Evaluation Kit: Glossary http://www.wmich.edu/evalctr/ess/glossary			■	

HUMAN RESOURCES

American Association of School Personnel Administrators

www.aaspa.com

ORGANIZATION DESCRIPTION. The American Association of School Personnel Administrators (AASPA) is a professional organization for school personnel and human resources staff. The purpose of the organization is to provide resources to members to help them work more effectively.

BENEFITS OF MEMBERSHIP. Members receive monthly publications, discounts on books, access to the members-only area of the Web site, a helpline service, and opportunities to participate in professional development activities.

SITE DESCRIPTION. Although much of the information available on the site is directly related to AASPA, nonmembers will find useful information in:

- **Career Net:** Job listings.

- **Publications:** A link to the AASPA Bookstore, where a variety of books and other documents arc available for purchase.

- **What's New:** Links to online information available to nonmembers.

HIGHLIGHTS FOR DISTRICT LEADERS. If you are looking for print materials on topics such as compensation, evaluation, job descriptions, or legal issues, the bookstore is a good place to start. A few free articles are available to nonmembers. Click on **What's New** to look at offerings such as *The Brief Case,* a collection of short articles on human resources issues.

HUMAN RESOURCES

Electronic Privacy Information Center

www.epic.org

SITE DESCRIPTION. Increased use of the Internet and e-mail has led to numerous questions and debate about employee rights and the appropriate limits of employer supervision. The Electronic Privacy Information Center (EPIC) is a public research information center that focuses on civil rights issues and privacy. The site offers information about court cases and legislation related to privacy in the Information Age.

HIGHLIGHTS FOR DISTRICT LEADERS. While there's a definite agenda here, the site is useful for finding information about court rulings and current cases that relate to various technologies and employee use. Read through back issues of *Epic Alert,* a free biweekly online newsletter, to see if a subscription would be helpful to you. Another way to find specific information on this site is to type a keyword (for example, "employees" or "teachers") into the Search EPIC.org text box, bringing up a list of related articles.

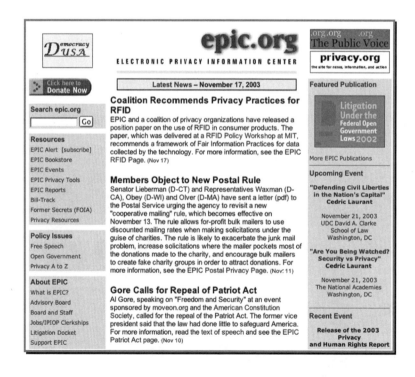

HUMAN RESOURCES

Social Security Online

www.ssa.gov

SITE DESCRIPTION. This site is very useful in navigating the Social Security and Medicare maze. While employees may still need to visit a local Social Security office to complete a transaction (e.g., a name change), using this site first helps with basic information and form completion.

HIGHLIGHTS FOR DISTRICT LEADERS. You can subscribe to Social Security's eNews updates for regular information about Social Security. Use the **Forms** link to access downloadable PDF files for all required forms. Find information about retirement benefits, Medicare, disability, and other benefits.

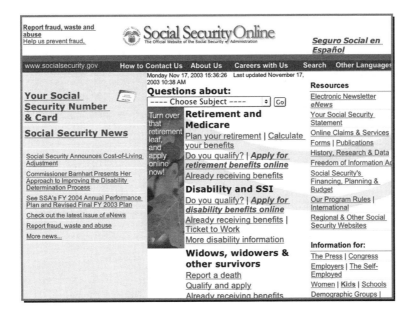

HUMAN RESOURCES

U.S. Department of Labor: Bureau of Labor Statistics
www.bls.gov

SITE DESCRIPTION. The U.S. Department of Labor: Bureau of Labor Statistics (BLS) Web site provides information about labor economics and statistics for wages and benefits, safety and health, employment rates, employment projections, and other information useful to the Personnel Department.

HIGHLIGHTS FOR DISTRICT LEADERS. Visit this site when preparing for negotiations with professional organizations, projecting future employment opportunities, or gathering other employment information for your community. For example, click on **Wages by Area and Occupation** to see how your district's pay scale stacks up regionally. Or, when writing a grant, use the **State and Local Unemployment Rates** link to find current employment statistics, useful for establishing need.

HUMAN RESOURCES

U.S. Equal Employment Opportunity Commission

www.eeoc.gov

SITE DESCRIPTION. Established in 1964, the U.S. Equal Employment Opportunity Commission (EEOC) deals with all forms of employment discrimination. The site features several important links:

- **Quick Start—Employees:** Selected documents related to employee rights and responsibilities.

- **Quick Start—Employers:** Selected documents related to employer rights and responsibilities.

- **Laws, Regulations, and Policy Guidance:** Information about laws enforced by the EEOC.

- **Publications:** Links to free documents and fact sheets published by the EEOC.

HIGHLIGHTS FOR DISTRICT LEADERS. All administrators need to be up to speed on employment discrimination issues. Use this Web site yourself, and share the URL with administrators throughout the district. No-cost education and outreach programs are available through the site, and you may want to look into hosting a meeting focused on employment issues.

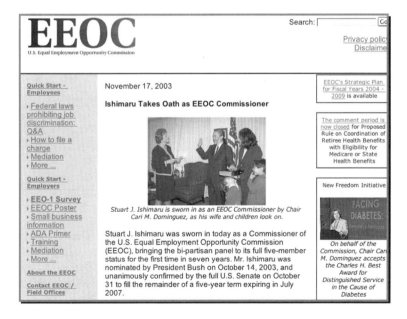

PROFESSIONAL DEVELOPMENT

e-Lead: Leadership for Student Learning

www.e-lead.org

SITE DESCRIPTION. The e-Lead site offers school districts a database of professional development programs and a library of resources. The primary focus of the site is high-quality professional development for school principals.

HIGHLIGHTS FOR DISTRICT LEADERS. This site offers a wealth of materials for district leaders designing a professional development program for school leaders, particularly principals. There are three main areas:

- **Professional Development Programming:** A summary of six research-based design principles for professional development programs for school leaders.

- **Programs Database:** A searchable database of exemplary professional development programs that incorporate the six design principles. Abstracts and full descriptions are provided for each program.

- **Leadership Library:** Links to articles, tools, and other resources for identifying content and planning professional development.

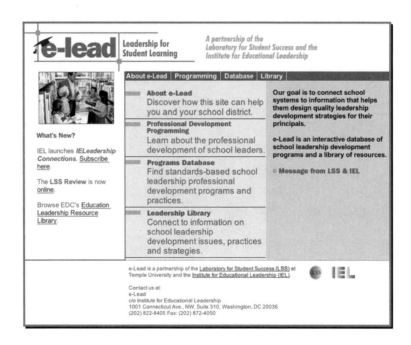

PROFESSIONAL DEVELOPMENT

National Staff Development Council

www.nsdc.org

ORGANIZATION DESCRIPTION. Founded in 1969, the National Staff Development Council (NSDC) is dedicated to school improvement through high-quality staff development programs.

BENEFITS OF MEMBERSHIP. There are three levels of membership. Individual members receive the *Journal of Staff Development* (quarterly) and either *Results* (eight issues annually) or *Tools for Schools* (bimonthly newsletter), the annual Conference Program, reduced conference fees, and a 20% discount on NSDC publications. Comprehensive individual members receive the same, plus subscriptions to both newsletters and access to members-only areas of the Web Site. Organizational members are entitled to all of the above, plus vouchers for three people to attend the conference at member rates.

SITE DESCRIPTION. These areas are of particular interest to district leaders:

- **Standards:** Twelve standards for designing effective staff development programs.
- **Library:** Extensive collection of articles from NSDC publications.
- **Powerful Words:** A collection of inspirational quotes on education.
- **Results-Based:** Three downloadable documents that describe effective, results-based staff development plans at K–12 schools.

HIGHLIGHTS FOR DISTRICT LEADERS. The NSDC standards for staff development and the result-based staff development documents can be used as a foundation for your professional development program. The **Library** articles are indispensable for committees engaged in professional development planning.

TEACHER QUALITY

ERIC Clearinghouse on Teaching and Teacher Education
www.ericsp.org/pages/about/index.html

SITE DESCRIPTION. The Educational Resources Information Center (ERIC) is a federally funded information network that provides access to literature on education. Currently, 16 centers across the nation acquire materials related to different aspects of education. ERIC may be reorganized into one large database in the near future. This link takes you to the Teaching and Teacher Education section. You can search the entire collection (organized into 12 major sections), read digests, and visit Web sites related to curriculum and instruction.

HIGHLIGHTS FOR DISTRICT LEADERS. The **Resources for Teachers** link takes you to an area where you can access education news, find downloadable publications about curriculum and instruction, and link to other content-related ERIC Clearinghouses. The **Digests and Publications** area offers links to a variety of online articles and summaries.

TEACHER QUALITY

National Board for Professional Teaching Standards

www.nbpts.org

SITE DESCRIPTION. The National Board for Professional Teaching Standards (NBPTS) site offers comprehensive information about all aspects of national board certification for educators. Helpful links include:

- **About NBPTS:** Comprehensive information about certification, including the history and rationale, available certificates, candidate recruitment, scholarship programs, and support.

- **Education Reform:** Success stories, a special area for school principals, and links to related Web sites.

- **Events, Calendar & Resources:** Use the **Products & Services** link to access documents about certification that can be downloaded.

- **News Center:** State and national news about certification.

- **Research & Information:** Current and archived research, as well as news items.

HIGHLIGHTS FOR DISTRICT LEADERS. As interest grows in national board certification for educators, it's important for district leaders to keep abreast of available certificates and requirements. Regular visits to this site, using the links described above, will keep you up-to-date on all aspects of national board certification.

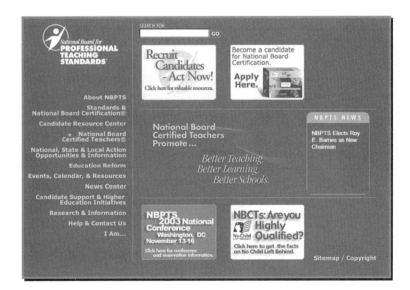

TEACHER QUALITY

National Governors Association: Teacher Quality

www.nga.org/center/topics/1,1188,D_401,00.html

SITE DESCRIPTION. The National Governors Association Center for Best Practices hosts this area on the National Governors Association Web site. The purpose of the information provided here is to keep governors and their staff up to date on policy issues related to teacher quality.

HIGHLIGHTS FOR DISTRICT LEADERS. Review the reports listed below the Latest Documents title. Current documents include information about No Child Left Behind (NCLB), mentoring, and teacher mobility. Links listed below Related Materials address topics such as recruiting and retaining teachers and redesigning teacher preparation programs.

TEACHER QUALITY

Teacher Evaluation: New Directions and Practices
www.teacherevaluation.net

SITE DESCRIPTION. This Web site was developed and is maintained by Kenneth D. Peterson, Ph.D., of Portland State University in Portland, Oregon. The site is updated bimonthly and addresses topics such as teacher hiring, new practices to improve teacher evaluation, improved roles for principals, and links to other online evaluation resources.

HIGHLIGHTS FOR DISTRICT LEADERS. This site isn't particularly slick, but there's some interesting information here. Click on the **New Web Site on Teacher Hiring** link to find a variety of resources, such as tips for interviewing, sample interview questions, and a **Bill of Rights for Teacher Hiring.** The **Essays** link leads to five short articles on various aspects of teacher evaluation.

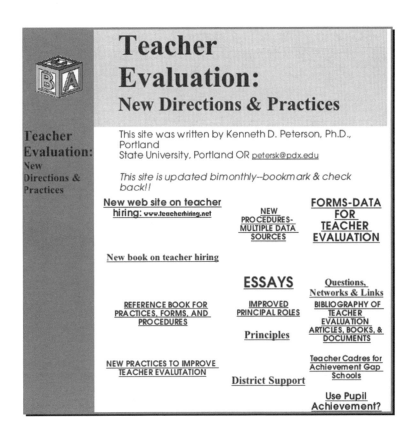

TEACHER QUALITY

Teacher Evaluation Kit: Glossary

http://www.wmich.edu/evalctr/ess/glossary

SITE DESCRIPTION. Developed by the Evaluation Center of Western Michigan University, this site provides an extensive glossary of terms related to teacher evaluation.

HIGHLIGHTS FOR DISTRICT LEADERS. Some misunderstandings that occur in the evaluation process are the result of a lack of common definitions for key terms. This glossary can be used to help administrators and staff come to a common understanding of the language of teacher evaluation.

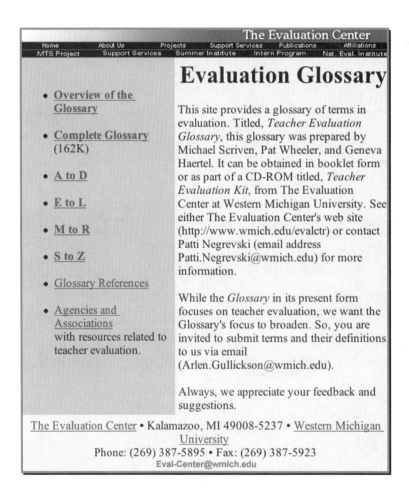

Social, Legal, and Ethical Issues

District leaders are charged with ensuring that staff and students abide by the laws and regulations that govern schools and districts. The six sites in this section offer information to assist you in helping staff and students follow copyright law, keep tabs on special education law, and explore ethics in education. You can also access court rulings and read about pending legal actions involving schools and districts.

Because each state has its own codes for education, no attempt is made here to address state law. Visit your state's department of education site for information. Access these sites by going to **http://bcol02.ed.gov/Programs/EROD/org_list.cfm?category_ID=SEA** and clicking on your state's listing. Or try a Google search by entering the name of your state and the words "Education Code" (for example, "Florida Education Code"). You might also want to visit the ERIC Clearinghouse on Educational Management at **www.eric.uoregon.edu.** Under the **Trends and Issues** area, you can find the topic **School Law.** More information about this site is provided in the Superintendent's Office section of this directory.

QUICK REFERENCE CHART

NAME OF SITE/INTERNET ADDRESS	PRIMARY AREA OF EMPHASIS			
	PROFESSIONAL ORGANIZATION	POLICY & LEGISLATION	PLANNING & ACTION	ONLINE JOURNAL
Copyright and Fair Use, Stanford University Libraries http://fairuse.stanford.edu		■	■	
Education Law Association www.educationlaw.org/links.htm	■	■		
FindLaw www.findlaw.com		■		
IDEAPractices www.ideapractices.org		■		
Markkula Center for Applied Ethics, Santa Clara University www.scu.edu/ethics		■		
Public Education Network (PEN) www.publiceducation.org		■	■	

Copyright and Fair Use, Stanford University Libraries

http://fairuse.stanford.edu

SITE DESCRIPTION. Advancing technologies make copyright infringement—both intentional and accidental—easier than ever before. School districts need to develop and enforce copyright policies to ensure that students and staff are following the law. This comprehensive site offers links to:

- **Primary Materials:** Including the **U.S. Constitution, U.S. Codes & Statutes, Recent U.S. Legislation,** and more.

- **Copyright & Fair Use Guide:** Links to Web sites, agencies, journals, and articles.

- **Key Copyright Sites:** Sites that explain copyright law such as Texas U's Copyright Crash Course.

- **Copyright & Fair Use Overview:** A helpful explanation of fair use.

- **Resources for Librarians:** Sample policies and links to organizations concerned with copyright issues.

- **Current Issues & Legislation:** Coverage of hot topics such as the **Digital Millennium Copyright Act** and the **TEACH Act.**

HIGHLIGHTS FOR DISTRICT LEADERS. Your district cannot afford to ignore this important issue. Get yourself up to speed on copyright law by taking the **Copyright Crash Course** yourself, and by reviewing the **Copyright & Fair Use Overview.** Check the information in **Current Issues & Legislation** against your own copyright policy to ensure that the policy is up to date.

Education Law Association

www.educationlaw.org/links.htm

ORGANIZATION DESCRIPTION. Affiliated with the University of Dayton's School of Education, the Education Law Association is an organization that focuses on understanding education law and the rights of employees, students, parents, and boards of education.

BENEFITS OF MEMBERSHIP. Members receive a one-year subscription to *ELA Notes* (four issues) and *School Reporter Law* (12 issues); discounts on publications, seminars, and conferences; and access to online services.

SITE DESCRIPTION. Nonmembers can download sample newsletters and access **Links** to a number of useful Web sites related to education law.

HIGHLIGHTS FOR DISTRICT LEADERS. Visit the **Links** area's **Legal Search Engines/Directories**. These listings are very helpful for district leaders trying to find Web sites that include information about education law.

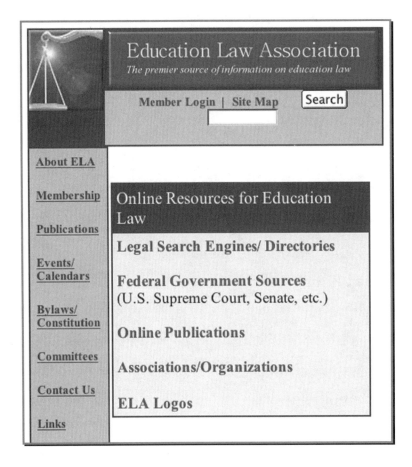

FindLaw

www.findlaw.com

SITE DESCRIPTION. This URL takes you to a directory page where you can find links to all sorts of legal issues. Use the Education link under **Public & Consumer Resources** for most of your needs. Under certain circumstances, links found under the **Business Resources** category (e.g., **Intellectual Property** or **Employer's Rights**) may also be useful.

HIGHLIGHTS FOR DISTRICT LEADERS. Click on **Articles** for access to information about general education law, special education law, discrimination and harassment, and more. The questions and answers in **Read Frequently Asked Questions** cover a broad range of topics, from homeschooling to religious activities in schools.

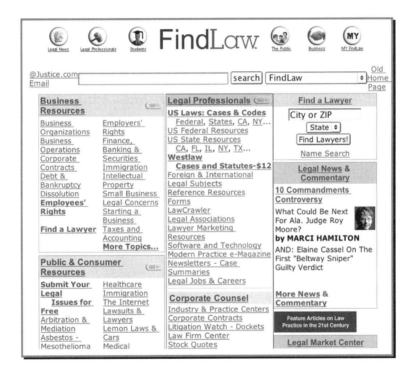

IDEAPractices

www.ideapractices.org

SITE DESCRIPTION. The purpose of the IDEAPractices Web site is to keep education professionals and families informed about IDEA (the Individuals with Disabilities Education Act) and to share successful strategies for compliance. The home page features popular resources and several links of interest to district leaders:

- **IDEAnews**
- **Law & Regulations**
- **Professional Development Resources**

HIGHLIGHTS FOR DISTRICT LEADERS. Sign up for the free monthly e-newsletter, IDEAnews. Then, browse the list of resources offered on the home page, including information about busing, assessment, and concerns for rural educators. The **Law & Regulations** area offers downloadable files of the IDEA law and associated regulations, as well as access to a link called **Litigation Log,** a collection of legal cases related to IDEA. The **Professional Development Resources** link leads you to a wide array of reading materials, such as articles and Web sites. Topics cover just about every imaginable area of IDEA compliance.

Markkula Center for Applied Ethics, Santa Clara University

www.scu.edu/ethics

SITE DESCRIPTION. Housed at Santa Clara University, the Markkula Center for Applied Ethics explores three areas that directly impact K–12 educators:

- **Character Education**
- **Technology Ethics**
- **Ethical Decision Making**

HIGHLIGHTS FOR DISTRICT LEADERS. The **Character Education** area focuses solely on K–12 education. Resources include articles, scenarios and dialogues (primarily aimed at high-school-aged students), and links to other Web sites. **Technology Ethics** and **Ethical Decision Making** encompass more than K–12 education but hit upon topics of concern to educators, including the digital divide, filtering, and employee privacy.

Public Education Network

www.publiceducation.org

SITE DESCRIPTION. This national association strongly supports public education and promotes school reform in low income areas through public demand and engagement in the reform process. The challenges tackled by the Public Education Network (PEN) often relate to social, legal, and ethical issues or concerns. The site includes links to publications, tools, and other online resources.

HIGHLIGHTS FOR DISTRICT LEADERS. Click on the **Tools/Publications** link to access guides, articles, and research reports. You can also subscribe to the free weekly e-newsletter, *NewsBlast*. Two recent free publications of interest to district leaders are a community guide to the No Child Left Behind legislation and a community guide to Teacher Quality.

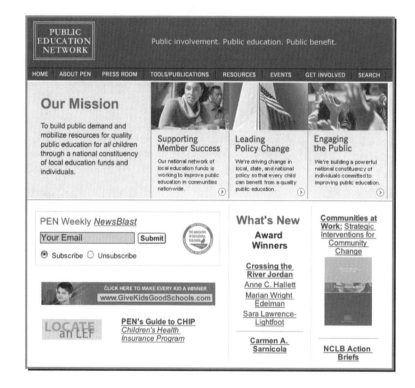

Superintendent's Office

While the superintendent and cabinet members are responsible for every department or division within the district office, there are special areas of interest that go beyond educational services, personnel, and business. The three focus areas in this section of the directory are:

- **Advocacy:** Featured sites provide up-to-date information about both U.S. Department of Education programs and initiatives and legislation that impacts education.

- **Leadership:** Sites listed here include the home page of a professional organization for school administrators, a clearinghouse for information about all aspects of education leadership, a site devoted to the special needs of big city schools, and a link to a professional publication.

- **Working With Boards of Education:** Featured sites include links to two professional organizations and a tool kit for educating board members about data-driven decision making.

NAME OF SITE/INTERNET ADDRESS	PRIMARY AREA OF EMPHASIS			
	PROFESSIONAL ORGANIZATION	POLICY & LEGISLATION	PLANNING & ACTION	ONLINE JOURNAL
ADVOCACY:				
Federal Register www.gpoaccess.gov/fr/		▓		
THOMAS: Legislative Information on the Internet http://thomas.loc.gov		▓		
U.S. Department of Education Mailing Lists www.ed.gov/MailingLists/		▓		▓
LEADERSHIP:				
American Association of School Administrators (AASA) www.aasa.org	▓			
Clearinghouse on Educational Policy and Management (CEPM) http://cepm.uoregon.edu/		▓	▓	
Council of the Great City Schools www.cgcs.org		▓	▓	
District Administration www.districtadministration.com				▓
WORKING WITH BOARDS OF EDUCATION:				
Improving School Board Decision Making: The Data Connection www.schoolboarddata.org			▓	
National Association of State Boards of Education (NASBE) www.nasbe.org	▓	▓		
National School Boards Association (NSBA) www.nsba.org	▓	▓		

ADVOCACY

Federal Register

www.gpoaccess.gov/fr/

SITE DESCRIPTION. The Federal Register publishes daily notices about rules, proposed rules, and executive orders and documents. Notices from governmental agencies, including program and grant information, are also published daily.

HIGHLIGHTS FOR DISTRICT LEADERS. Find information by searching records back to 1994. You can also scroll down to **Other Services** and sign up for a daily e-newsletter that provides the Federal Register Table of Contents.

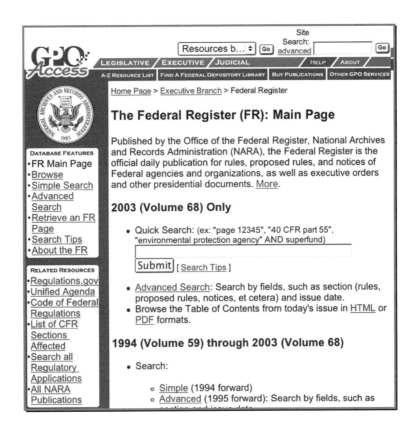

ADVOCACY

THOMAS: Legislative Information on the Internet

http://thomas.loc.gov

SITE DESCRIPTION. Updated daily, this Web site provides the full text of bills currently under consideration in both chambers of Congress. It also provides summaries and status, committee information, measures expected to be considered each week, and more.

HIGHLIGHTS FOR DISTRICT LEADERS. When looking for information on a specific bill, type the bill number or key words into the search box at the top of the home page. If you're curious about education bills in general, click on **Bill Summary & Status** or **Committee Reports,** then select education-related titles from the drop-down menus that appear in the search boxes.

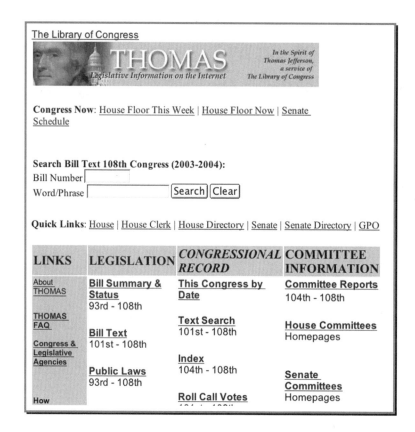

ADVOCACY

U.S. Department of Education Mailing Lists

www.ed.gov/MailingLists/

SITE DESCRIPTION. An efficient way to keep tabs on programs offered by the U.S. Department of Education is to sign up for one or more free e-newsletters. This Web page provides links to subscription forms for e-newsletters currently available.

HIGHLIGHTS FOR DISTRICT LEADERS. Three e-newsletters are being published at this time. *EDInfo* provides general news from the Department of Education. *EDTV* sends updates about broadcasts of television programs designed to educate parents about No Child Left Behind. The *OESE Listserv* comes from the Office of Elementary and Secondary Education and focuses on K–12 education.

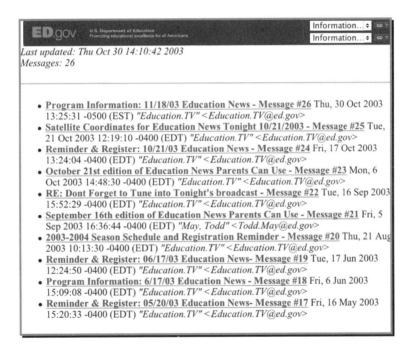

LEADERSHIP

American Association of School Administrators

www.aasa.org

ORGANIZATION DESCRIPTION. Founded in 1865, the American Association of School Administrators (AASA) offers support to K–12 school district administrators.

BENEFITS OF MEMBERSHIP. This site provides access to AASA's online Network Program, special interest groups for AASA members, a subscription to *The School Administrator,* reduced rates for conferences and other events, advocacy activities, discounts on books and other materials, and a legal support program.

SITE DESCRIPTION. Although much of the information available on the site is directly related to AASA, nonmembers will find useful information in:

- **Government Relations:** Information about funding, the Individuals With Disabilities Edcuation Act, the No Child Left Behind Act, rural issues, and other federal topics.

- **Issues and Insights:** Articles, reports, and Web sites related to various topics such as assessment or community involvement.

- **Publications:** Links to online versions of *The School Administrator* and *School Governance & Leadership.*

HIGHLIGHTS FOR DISTRICT LEADERS. Check out the online versions of *The School Administrator* and *School Governance & Leadership.* Both publications directly serve the needs and interests of district leaders. Save research time by taking advantage of the wealth of information available in **Issues and Insights**.

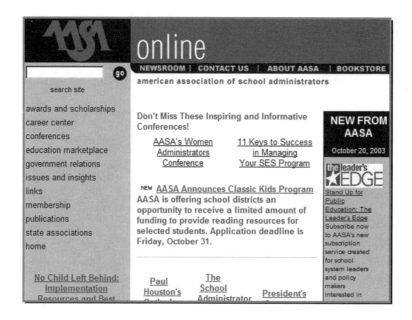

LEADERSHIP

Clearinghouse on Educational Policy and Management
http://www.cepm.ed.gov

SITE DESCRIPTION. The Clearinghouse on Educational Policy and Management (CEPM) is operated by the College of Education at the University of Oregon. Until 2004, the site operated as an ERIC Clearinghouse, a federally funded information network that provides access to literature on education. This link lets you access resources produced by the ERIC Clearinghouse on Educational Management. Here you can browse titles in content areas such as:

- Trends & Issues

- Hot Topics

- Publications

- Directory of Organizations

- Links

HIGHLIGHTS FOR DISTRICT LEADERS. You'll want to share this site with members of your cabinet and management team, as well as visit it regularly yourself. The home page features what's new in each section of the Web site, providing links for quick access. To access all information, scroll down the home page and review the different topics listed for each section, then click on a title to explore that topic in greater detail.

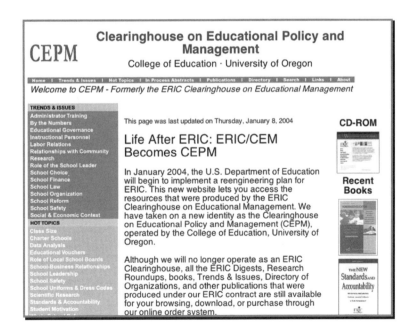

LEADERSHIP

Council of the Great City Schools

www.cgcs.org

SITE DESCRIPTION. The Council of the Great City Schools is a coalition of the 60 largest school districts in America. The council promotes improved quality of urban education through projects, advocacy, research, media relations, and other strategies.

HIGHLIGHTS FOR DISTRICT LEADERS. Visit the **Reports & Data** area of the Web site to find information on urban schools, professional development, bilingual education, finance, leadership and governance, and more. Reports can be downloaded for free, or bound copies may be purchased through the Web site. The **Urban Educator** link leads to current and back issues of the council's journal. Again, articles are available for download. To learn about the council's advocacy activities, click on **Legislative Services.**

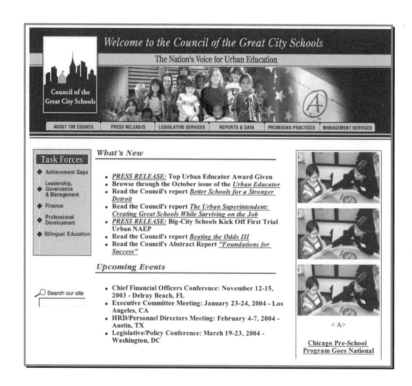

LEADERSHIP

District Administration

www.districtadministration.com

SITE DESCRIPTION. This is the online version of the print magazine. This publication targets superintendents and cabinet-level leaders, but good information is available for district leaders at other levels as well. The Web site offers current education news from national newspapers, articles from current and past issues of the magazine, and access to special reports.

HIGHLIGHTS FOR DISTRICT LEADERS. Sign up to receive the **District Daily e-newsletter.** This free service delivers breaking education news to your e-mail in-box each business day. Use the **Current Issue** and **Back Issues** links to find feature articles, columns, and updates. If you like what you read, you can also sign up for a free subscription to the print magazine using the **Subscribe to District Administrator magazine** link.

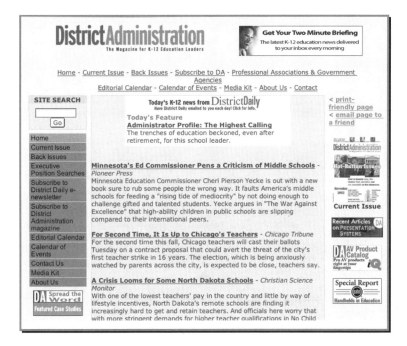

WORKING WITH BOARDS OF EDUCATION

Improving School Board Decision Making: The Data Connection
www.schoolboarddata.org

SITE DESCRIPTION. In this time of increased accountability, it's important that superintendents ensure that school board members understand how to engage in data-driven decision making. This Web site provides a book published by the National School Boards Foundation (available in PDF format), PowerPoint presentations suitable for training sessions, and other materials and support documentation to use when working with school board members.

HIGHLIGHTS FOR DISTRICT LEADERS. Download and read the book first. The links on the left side of the home page provide supporting information and materials for each chapter of the book. Topics include: **Dealing with Data, Setting Community Goals, What Data Measures,** and **Informing Board Decision Making.**

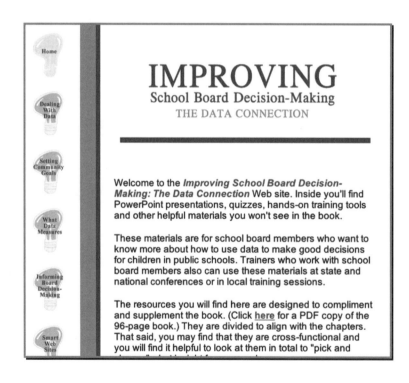

WORKING WITH BOARDS OF EDUCATION

National Association of State Boards of Education

www.nasbe.org

ORGANIZATION DESCRIPTION. The National Association of State Boards of Education (NASBE) is a professional organization for members of state boards of education, as well as other interested parties.

BENEFITS OF MEMBERSHIP. District administrators are invited to join NASBE as associate members. Members receive free publications, invitations to participate in professional development activities, and access to the members-only area of the Web site.

SITE DESCRIPTION. Areas of interest for superintendents include:

- **Education Issues:** Downloadable reports, articles, and policy briefs.
- **No Child Left Behind:** Links to state guidelines and news, NASBE information, and U.S. Department of Education resources.
- **Healthy Schools:** Publications, state-level health initiatives, and sample health policies.
- **Links to State Education Agencies**

HIGHLIGHTS FOR DISTRICT LEADERS. Sign up for one or more of NASBE's free e-newsletters. Plan to spend some time visiting the **Education Issues, No Child Left Behind**, and **Healthy Schools** areas.

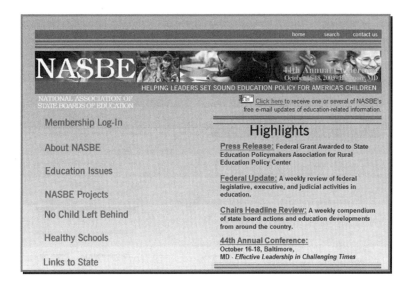

WORKING WITH BOARDS OF EDUCATION

National School Boards Association

www.nsba.org

ORGANIZATION DESCRIPTION. Founded in 1940, the National School Boards Association (NSBA) is a professional organization for members of school boards, as well as other interested parties.

BENEFITS OF MEMBERSHIP. School districts can join as national affiliates. Benefits include print resources, such as *School Board News;* legislative alerts; access to members-only areas of the Web site; and discounts on publications and conference registration.

SITE DESCRIPTION. Areas of interest to district leaders include:

- **Advocacy & Legislation:** Legislative issues and weekly news from Capitol Hill.

- **School Governance:** Topics related to the role school boards play in local governance, helping leaders to bridge the gap between the school system and the community.

- **School Law:** News, issues, and updates.

- **Publications & Reports**: Downloadable reports and articles.

HIGHLIGHTS FOR DISTRICT LEADERS. The home page highlights articles in current issues of the *American School Board Journal* and *School Board News,* along with new tools and resources posted on the site. **Weekly News on Capitol Hill** (found in the **Advocacy & Legislation** area) is a point-and-click tool that enables you to quickly access legislation updates. While visiting the **School Law** area, you may want to subscribe to *Legal Clips,* a free weekly e-newsletter offering updates on important legal issues related to education. The **School Law Issues** area contains resources and case citations for many topics, including technology, curriculum, and athletics.

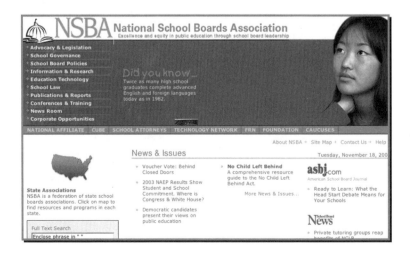

PART 2

INTERNET SURVIVAL SKILLS

CHAPTER 1
Hardware and
Connections

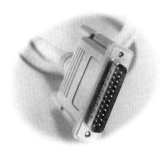

CHAPTER 2
Internet and
World Wide Web
Basics

CHAPTER 3
Beyond the Basics

INTRODUCTION TO PART 2

Please note: Chapters 1 and 2 of part 2 are designed to help beginning Internet users get online successfully. Seasoned Internet users who are helping fellow principals learn about the Internet may want to use the material here as a guide. If you are interested in learning more advanced Internet skills, refer to part 2, chapter 3.

My goal is to encourage district leaders to use the Internet, a powerful source of information and ideas that can make the district administrator's job more manageable. However, my experience working with school administrators tells me that principals often do not take advantage of Internet resources. This happens for a variety of reasons, but usually it boils down to three factors:

- hardware issues, including inadequate computer equipment or a slow Internet connection

- software problems due to a lack of familiarity with Web browsers, search engines, and the like

- lack of familiarity with information and resources available online

When your computer equipment isn't up to snuff or you don't understand how to use the software provided to get around the Internet and World Wide Web, you can waste a lot of time—not an attractive proposition for most district leaders. Just one or two unhappy experiences are enough to deter many district leaders from using the Internet in their professional lives. Much of this difficulty can be avoided, or at least significantly reduced, with basic information about equipment and software.

The information provided in chapter 1, Hardware and Connections, and chapter 2, Internet and World Wide Web Basics, will help you access the Web sites listed in the book's Web site directory. Chapter 3 contains information for more advanced users. Here is a brief summary of the three chapters.

- **Chapter 1—Hardware and Connections** deals with the physical setup you need to actually get online. If you already have this capability at home and are happy with your connection speed, move on to chapter 2. If you will be accessing the Internet through a high-speed connection at the office, again skip to chapter 2. However, if you are just getting set up to go online at the office or home, are using a telephone line for your connection, or don't have a clue what this paragraph means, you need to start with chapter 1. The material here won't make you a tech guru, but it will provide the information you need to get started.

- **Chapter 2—Internet and World Wide Web Basics** explains how to get online and the basics for accessing Web sites once you're connected to the Internet. A section is included that identifies common problems new Internet users face, with simple remedies so that your time spent online is productive and satisfying.

- **Chapter 3—Beyond the Basics** is for readers who want to use more than one Internet browser, work with multiple browsing windows, and organize and maintain lists of favorites or bookmarked sites. Information about how to conduct productive Internet searches to find additional Web sites is also provided.

CHAPTER 1

Hardware and Connections

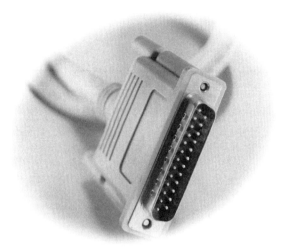

Will you be using the Internet at the office? At home? Both? Your equipment, connection, and Internet service provider (ISP) needs will be different at each location. Due to E-Rate, many districts now offer computer networks where Internet access is available through a high-speed connection. If this is true in your district, you don't need to worry about basic hardware and connection issues at work. However, if your district does not have a network and a high-speed connection or if you want to access the Internet from home, read on.

The information presented here assumes you are considering an Internet connection from home, just to keep things simple. However, if you need a telephone connection to the Internet at school, the advice still applies.

To get online using a stand-alone computer, your *minimum* needs are:

- a computer
- a modem
- a telephone line
- an ISP

COMPUTER

Today's Web sites make heavy use of graphics, sound, animation, and text. Newer computers are better equipped to handle these sites because they have faster processors, contain more memory, and manage graphics well. You do not need a crash course on computer specifications, but you do want to use a computer that is capable of handling the Web pages you want to access. If your computer is less than three years old, you should be fine. If your computer is older, you may have difficulty.

Seek advice from your district computer technician. Write down the make and model of your computer system or bring your owner's manual when you meet. Explain that you are interested in using the Internet in your work and ask whether your current computer system is up to the job. If it is, the technician can quickly ascertain this. If not, he or she may be able to recommend inexpensive upgrades that would allow you to successfully access the Internet. If your computer is too old to upgrade, you may need to purchase a newer model before you can use the Internet easily from home.

In that case, if you have an adequate setup at the office, I'd recommend that you first spend some time learning how to access Web sites there. Getting some Internet experience under your belt using district equipment can help you decide whether you actually want to make an investment in a new computer or other equipment for home use.

VOCABULARY TERM

modem
Stands for **mo**dulator-**dem**odulator. This device may be external (outside your computer) or internal (usually a card plugged into a slot inside your computer). The modem converts data stored on your computer into a format that can be transferred via telephone or cable lines. Different modems send and receive data at different speeds. Generally, the faster the better.

MODEM

The modem is a device that enables your computer to communicate with the Internet. If your home computer does not already have a modem, the computer itself is probably too old and slow for today's Internet demands. New computers typically come with at least a V.90 56K modem installed. (The numbers refer to the speed of data transfer.) This modem enables you to use a regular telephone line to connect with the Internet.

Although it's possible to do so, you do not want to use a modem with a top speed that is less than 56K, because data transmission will slow to a crawl. If your current modem's top speed capability is less than 56K, talk with your technician about options for replacing it.

If you decide to use a different type of connection, such as cable or DSL, the company you contract with will provide a special modem for you to use, even if you have a V.90 56K modem. This special modem will require installation. It is worth your while to pay the installation fee and have the company install it for you.

TELEPHONE LINE

You can use your existing telephone line to access the Internet. This is called a dial-up connection. The advantage is that it doesn't cost more to do this, unless you have to make a toll or long-distance call to your Internet service provider. However, there are disadvantages. Using your existing telephone line means you can't make voice calls when someone in your home is logged on to the Internet, unless you install a second phone line. Also, data transmission over voice lines is slow. Because of this, it's not uncommon for users to be disconnected while attempting to access Web pages. Educators I work with who use dial-up connections frequently express frustration about slow-loading Web sites, being knocked offline, and other problems.

VOCABULARY TERMS

DSL
Short for digital subscriber lines. DSL offers subscribers a high-speed Internet connection through telephone lines. DSL is not available in all areas, and access depends on the subscriber's proximity to telephone switching stations.

cable modem
A modem designed to send and receive data through television cable networks. Data transmission speed is very fast, but the technology is still being refined. Cable Internet service is not available in all areas or through all cable companies.

In many areas, it is now possible to connect to the Internet from home using DSL or a cable connection. Each option is fairly inexpensive (as little as $50/month), and both provide much faster service than a dial-up connection. Even though a DSL connection uses your telephone line, you can still make and receive voice calls while online. Another advantage of DSL or cable is that you do not need to pay an additional fee for a commercial Internet service provider because these services connect you directly to the Internet. When you factor in the cost of maintaining a second phone line, DSL and cable aren't much more expensive than a dial-up connection. They also offer e-mail services to customers.

VOCABULARY TERM

ISP

Short for Internet service provider. These companies provide access to the Internet for a monthly fee. A dial-up connection to the Internet requires that a user go through some sort of ISP to access the Internet.

INTERNET SERVICE PROVIDER

If you are using a dial-up connection, you must have a separate account with an Internet service provider to access the Internet. (This service is included when you have a DSL or cable connection because your computer connects directly to the Internet each time you turn it on.) When you sign up for an ISP account, you receive software, a user name, a password, and an access telephone number. Once the software is installed on your computer, it's usually simple to follow the directions provided to log on to the Internet. Your ISP should offer voice technical assistance in case you encounter any problems getting online. Write down the help line telephone number and keep it next to your computer.

Well-known commercial ISPs include America Online or Earthlink. It is often possible to pick up a free copy of ISP software at a retail electronics store, install the software, and open your account online.

Unless you live in an isolated area, you should be able to find an ISP that offers its customers a local access number. This is important. If you must use a number that is a long-distance call, your telephone bill will reflect these charges, which mount up very quickly. New Internet users who do not understand about telephone charges have accrued enormous telephone bills.

Internet and World Wide Web Basics

N ow that you have the necessary hardware, modem, and connection in place, and you have acquired an ISP account, the next step is actually getting on to the Internet. Because there are Windows and Macintosh versions of commonly used browsers, separate directions are given for PCs and Macintosh. Read through the introductory material first, and then continue with the section of this chapter that matches your system.

Although people often use the terms *Internet* and *World Wide Web* interchangeably, as you can see in the definitions provided here, they really aren't synonymous.

VOCABULARY TERMS

Internet
The Internet provides the network infrastructure that enables millions of computers around the world to connect to one another for communication purposes.

World Wide Web
The World Wide Web is one source of information for Internet users, but it is not the Internet itself. It uses the Internet network to allow people to access Web sites.

Once you have established a connection to the Internet, you use a Web browser to actually view Web sites.

VOCABULARY TERM

Web browser
A software application (program) used to access Web pages. Some ISPs (America Online, for example) provide their own Web browser. Other ISPs use commonly available Web browsers, usually Internet Explorer or Netscape Communicator. Most newer computer systems come with Internet Explorer or Netscape Communicator already installed.

WHAT IS A WEB BROWSER?

When using a dial-up connection, you first connect to the Internet through your ISP, then use the Web browser provided by your ISP to navigate the Web. A DSL, cable, or other high-speed connection is a bit different. Steps to get online are provided here for both dial-up and high-speed connections.

DIRECTIONS FOR USING A PC AND WINDOWS

Note: If you use a Macintosh computer, skip to page 153.

Logging on using a dial-up connection

Please note: The figures here show America Online as an example, but these directions work with other commercial Internet service providers and browsers.

1. Turn on your computer.

2. Find the icon for your ISP software on the computer desktop (Figure 1). Open the software by double-clicking on the icon.

FIGURE 1. Finding your ISP software shortcut.

If you do not see an icon on your desktop, click on Start in the Windows Taskbar. Scroll up to highlight Programs. A pop-up menu listing all programs installed on your computer will appear. Highlight the name of your ISP software and double-click (Figure 2).

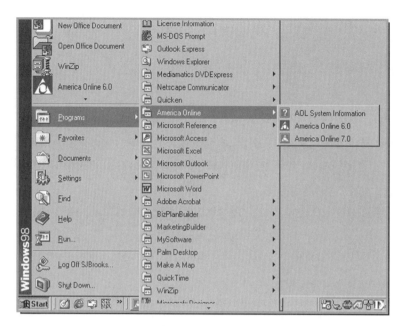

FIGURE 2. Using Start and Programs to find your ISP program.

3. Once the ISP software is open, a sign-on or connect window will open. Click once on the sign-on button. The software will connect you to the Internet through your ISP (Figure 3).

FIGURE 3. Example of a sign-on screen.

VOCABULARY TERM

home page

The main page of a Web site.

---

4. When the Internet connection is made, you will see the home page for your ISP (Figure 4).

FIGURE 4. Example of an ISP home page.

Logging on using a DSL, cable, or other high-speed connection

1. If you are using a DSL, cable, or other high-speed connection, simply turn on the computer and modem and you will be connected to the Internet.

2. Although your computer is already connected to the Internet, to actually view sites you need to look on your computer's desktop for a Web browser icon, such as Internet Explorer or Netscape Communicator. Open the software by double-clicking on the icon (Figure 5).

FIGURE 5. This desktop shows icons for two different Web browsers, Internet Explorer and Netscape Communicator. To open either program, double-click on the icon.

If you do not see an icon on your desktop, click on Start in the Windows Taskbar. Scroll up to highlight Programs. A pop-up menu listing all programs installed on your computer will appear. Highlight the name of your Web browser software and double-click (Figure 6).

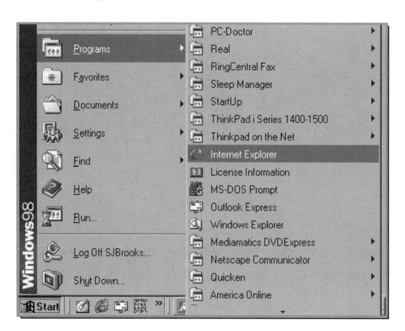

FIGURE 6. Using Start and Programs to find your Web browser program.

3. After opening the Web browser, you will see its home page (Figure 7).

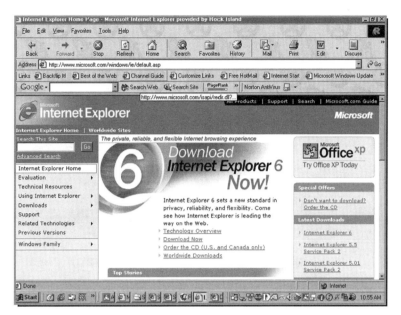

FIGURE 7. Example of a Web browser home page through a high-speed connection.

Using a Web browser

Overview of the Web browser window

Although there are different Web browsers, the windows are remarkably similar in design. For the sake of simplicity, the following figures and discussion use Internet Explorer 6 as an example. However, the information presented is applicable to Web browsers in general. Figure 8 identifies the common toolbars found on a Web browser window.

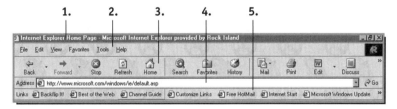

FIGURE 8. Internet Explorer toolbars.

1. **Title bar.** The name of the Web page that is open appears here.

2. **Menu bar.** These drop-down menus have commands for using all of the program's features.

3. **Standard toolbar.** The buttons on this toolbar provide the basic tools you need to use the Web browser.

4. **Address bar.** This is where you type addresses for Web sites.

5. **Links bar.** These are direct links to sites of interest. The default sites are Microsoft-related, but you can customize the bar with your own special links.

In addition to the toolbars, there are other features of the Web browser window that you will want to use. Figure 9 points out these features.

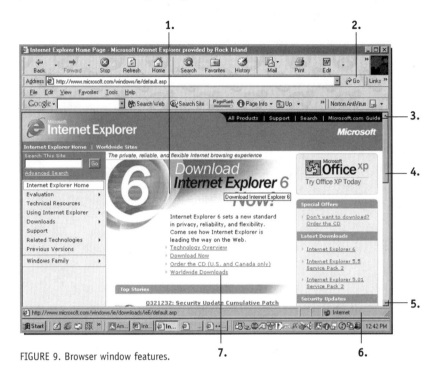

FIGURE 9. Browser window features.

1. **Browsing window.** This is the area where Web pages are displayed.

2. **Go button.** When a Web site address is typed in the address window, clicking the Go button takes you to the site.

3. **Scroll-up arrow.** Click on this arrow to scroll up the page displayed in the browsing window.

4. **Scroll bar.** Click and drag the box here to move up or down the page displayed in the browsing window.

5. **Scroll-down arrow.** Click on this arrow to scroll down the page displayed in the browsing window.

6. **Connectivity icon.** When you see this icon, it indicates that you are online.

7. **Link.** Links are very powerful. They enable you to move from one Web page to another. Links appear as text or graphics. To find a link, move your cursor across the browsing window. Whenever the cursor changes to a hand icon, it is pointing at a link. Text links are usually easy to identify because the text will be underlined and a different color. To access a link and view additional pages, click when the hand icon appears.

Understanding Web site addresses

The anatomy of a Web site address

Before learning more about browser tools, it's important to understand the structure of Web site addresses, or URLs. This is because you use the browser tools in conjunction with the Web site addresses you enter into the address bar. Web site addresses are often confusing to work with if you don't understand the naming conventions.

VOCABULARY TERMS

URL

An abbreviation for Uniform Resource Locator. Every file on the Internet has a unique address, or URL, assigned to it so you can find the file. URLs have two parts. The first part identifies the protocol or format of the file. Web page URLs usually begin with "http." The second part of the URL is the domain name, which identifies where the Web page you want is stored.

domain name

A domain name is part of an Internet address or URL.

Let's take a closer look at an actual URL (Figure 10).

FIGURE 10. Sample URL.

1. **Protocol.** This identifies the format of the file you are accessing. Most Web pages begin with http://. There are two other protocols you may encounter.

   - **https://** indicates a secure Web site where steps have been taken to protect data.

   - **ftp://** means file transfer protocol and indicates that a file has been uploaded on an ftp server. This file can be downloaded in full by a computer that accesses the ftp address.

Parts 2–4 comprise the domain name. Here's what each part means:

2. **www.** This stands for World Wide Web. Most, but not all, URLs include this.

3. **Host.** This identifies the owner of the Web site. In the example above, "ISTE" tells you that the International Society for Technology in Education owns the Web site.

4. **Domain suffix.** This part of the URL is very important because it provides information about the origin of a Web page. You can use this information to help determine the credibility of a Web page. There are a limited number of suffixes. The most common are:

- **gov**   government

- **edu**   education

- **org**   organization

- **com**   commercial

- **net**   network

- **mil**   military

The domain suffix of **org** in the sample URL tells you that ISTE is an organization.

How can you use this information to determine site credibility? Look at the two imaginary Internet addresses below:

- **http://www.excellentuniversity.edu**

- **http://www.excellentuniversity.com**

Which address is more likely to be legitimate? Probably the address ending in **edu**, because this tells you it is an educational institution. The address ending in **com** tells you this is a commercial site.

Many of the URLs you find in this directory will have additional information beyond the domain suffix. This is because the address through the suffix takes you to the Web site home page. The additional information will take you further into the site, bypassing the home page. For example, the URL **http://www.census.gov/govs/www/school.html** takes you beyond the home page for the Census Bureau (**http://www.census.gov**), directly to a document titled *Federal, State, and Local Governments Public Elementary-Secondary Education Finance Data.*

Entering a URL

To enter a new URL, you must first clear the URL already in the address bar. Do this by pointing at the URL and clicking once. This will highlight the existing URL (Figure 11).

FIGURE 11. Highlighting an existing URL.

When the existing URL is highlighted, you can begin typing the new Web address. Be very careful as you type the address. Include all punctuation marks and check the spelling. The URL must be entered exactly to successfully access the Web site.

If you make a mistake, you can click once to highlight the text in the address bar and start over. You can also correct an error by pointing at the mistake and clicking twice. This causes a flashing cursor to appear in the address bar where you have pointed. You can then edit the URL by using the backspace (or delete) key and retyping. Editing a URL uses the same techniques you use to edit in a word-processing document.

Once the URL is correctly typed, press Enter or click on the Go button to access the new Web site (Figure 12).

FIGURE 12. Go button.

You need to wait for the Web page to download before you can read it. This is when the speed of your connection becomes important. A dial-up connection takes much longer to download a site, especially if there are many graphics.

Occasionally you will have difficulty opening a Web page. You may see a message that the page cannot be displayed. Check to make sure you typed the URL correctly. If you made a mistake, retype or edit the URL and try again. If the URL appears to be correct, it's possible that the site is temporarily down, that the URL has been changed, or that the page is no longer available. Wait awhile and try the URL again. If you continue to get the error message, read and follow the directions that appear with the message. They will take you to the site's home page, where you may be able to find the specific information you need.

Essential Web browser tools

Now that you have opened a Web page, you need to know about the tools you can use to navigate the site and save or print information. Look closely at Figure 13. You see 12 tool buttons here. Although you may want to learn more about all the buttons on this bar, to get started you really only need to use four: Back, Forward, Favorites, and Print.

FIGURE 13. Essential Web browser tools.

Back and Forward

A common experience for new Internet users is to follow several links in a Web site and suddenly become "lost," not understanding how to retrace their steps to return to a previous page. There are several ways to move back and forth between pages you've visited using the Back and Forward buttons.

The simplest way to go back and forth is to move page by page. You can do this by clicking on the Back or Forward buttons. Each click moves one page forward or backward, depending on which button you choose (Figure 14).

FIGURE 14. Back and Forward buttons.

The appearance of the buttons tells you whether there are pages to move to. For example, in Figure 14, the Back button is gray and the label is in black text (active), indicating there are Web pages that can be moved back to, but the shadowy appearance (inactive) of the Forward arrow and label indicates there are no pages currently to move forward to. Therefore, at this time the Web page displayed is the last page visited during this session.

Now look at the small arrowheads just to the right of each tool button in Figure 14. By clicking on the darkened arrowhead to the right of the Back button, you can see a list of the sites you have visited during your current online session. Figure 15 illustrates this.

FIGURE 15. Sample Back list accessed through a drop-down menu.

Highlight a site name in the drop-down list and click. You will be taken directly to that page.

If you have moved back to a previous page and then decide to revisit a page you just left, use the arrowhead to the right of the Forward button. Figure 16 illustrates this.

FIGURE 16. Sample Forward list accessed through a drop-down menu.

In this example, there are three pages the user can choose to move forward to by highlighting the site name and clicking.

Favorites

You will find Web sites that you want to revisit at a later time. This means you cannot access them from the Back and Forward drop-down menus because these include only those sites accessed during the current online session. You could keep a hand-written list of sites next to your computer, but then you would need to worry about copying URLs accurately and not losing the list!

Fortunately, Web browsers provide an option that allows you to make a list of sites you want to go back to later. Some browsers call this "bookmarking," but in Internet Explorer it's called "Favorites." By clicking on the Favorites button in the tool bar, you open a column on the left side of your browser window (Figure 17). There is a button here that allows you to add a site to the list. You can also scroll through the list, high-light the name of a site, and click. This takes you directly to that site.

FIGURE 17. Using Favorites tools.

1. **Favorites button.** This button acts like a toggle switch. Click it once and the Favorites list will appear on the left side of your screen. Click it again, and the Favorites list will be hidden.

2. **Close button.** Another tool you can use to close the Favorites list when you aren't working with it.

3. **Add button.** When you are visiting a site you'd like to add to your Favorites list, click on this button and follow the simple directions that appear.

4. **Favorites list.** This is the list of sites you can save and visit time after time. Most browsers come installed with certain sites already included in the list. You can use the Favorites drop-down menu on the menu bar to delete unwanted sites.

Print

There are times you will want to print a site page instead of making it a Favorite. Perhaps you want specific information but doubt that you would want to visit the site again at a later time. Printing the Web page that is currently in the browsing window is easy. Simply click on the Print button in the toolbar (Figure 18).

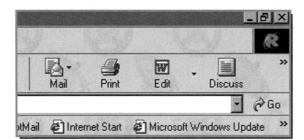

FIGURE 18. Print button on toolbar.

DIRECTIONS FOR USING A MACINTOSH

Logging on using a dial-up connection

Please note: The figures in this first section show America Online as an example, but these directions work with other commercial Internet service provider browsers.

1. Turn on your computer.

2. Find the icon for your ISP software on the computer desktop (Figure 19). Open the software by double-clicking on the icon.

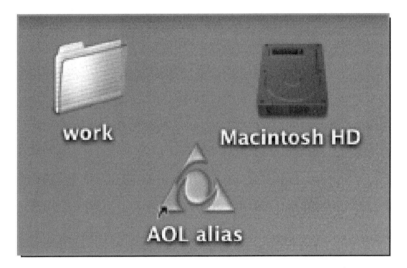

FIGURE 19. This desktop shows an icon for the ISP America Online. To open the program, move the pointer to the icon and double-click.

If you do not see an icon on your desktop, double-click on the hard drive icon on your desktop. You will see folders for information stored on your hard drive, including one called Applications. Open the Applications folder by double-clicking. An icon for America Online will appear, if it is installed on your computer. Double-click on the icon to open the program (Figures 20 and 21).

FIGURE 20. Looking at your hard drive to find your Applications folder.

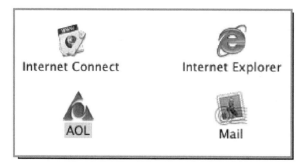

FIGURE 21. Finding the AOL icon in the Applications folder.

3. Once the ISP software is open, a sign-on or connect window will open. Enter your password and click once on the sign-on button. The software will connect you to the Internet through your ISP (Figure 22).

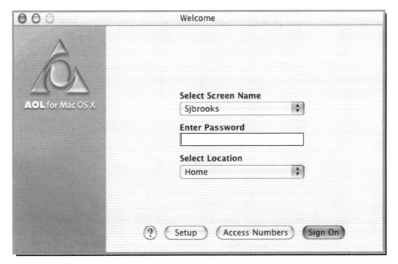

FIGURE 22. Example of a sign-on screen.

VOCABULARY TERM

home page

The main page of a Web site.

4. When the Internet connection is made, you will see the home page for your ISP (Figure 23).

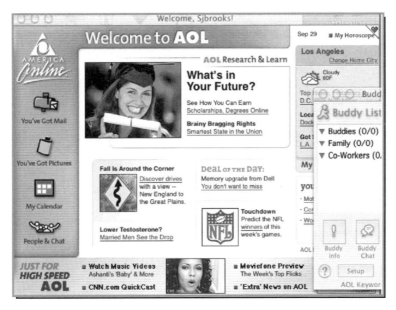

FIGURE 23. Example of an ISP home page.

Logging on using a DSL, cable, or other high-speed connection

1. If you are using a DSL, cable, or other high-speed connection, simply turn on the computer and modem and you will be connected to the Internet.

2. Although your computer is already connected to the Internet, to actually view sites you need to look on your computer's desktop for a Web browser icon, such as Internet Explorer or Netscape Communicator. Open the software by double-clicking on the icon (Figure 24).

FIGURE 24. An icon for Internet Explorer. To open the program, double-click on the icon.

If you do not see an icon anywhere on your desktop, double-click on the hard drive icon on your desktop. You will see folders for various programs and files stored on your hard drive. You should see a folder called Applications. Double-click on the Applications folder to open it, then double-click on the Internet Explorer icon to open the program (Figures 25 and 26).

FIGURE 25. Looking at your hard drive to find your Applications folder.

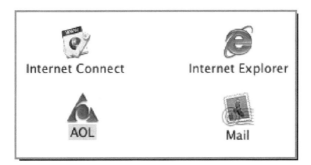

FIGURE 26. Finding the Internet Explorer icon in the Applications folder.

3. After opening the Web browser, you will see its home page (Figure 27).

FIGURE 27. Example of a Web browser home page through a high-speed connection.

Using a Web browser

Overview of the Web browser window

Although there are different Web browsers, the windows are remarkably similar in design. For the sake of simplicity, the following figures and discussion use Internet Explorer 5 as an example. However, the information presented is applicable to Web browsers in general. Figure 28 identifies the common toolbars found on a Web browser window.

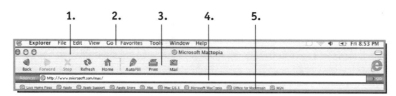

FIGURE 28. Internet Explorer toolbars.

1. **Title bar.** The name of the Web page that is open appears here.

2. **Menu bar.** These drop-down menus have commands for using all of the program's features.

3. **Standard toolbar.** The buttons on this toolbar provide the basic tools you need to use the Web browser.

4. **Address bar.** This is where you type addresses for Web sites.

5. **Links bar.** These are direct links to sites of interest. The default sites are Microsoft-related, but you can customize the bar with your own special links.

In addition to the toolbars, there are other features of the Web browser window that you will want to use. Figure 29 points out these features.

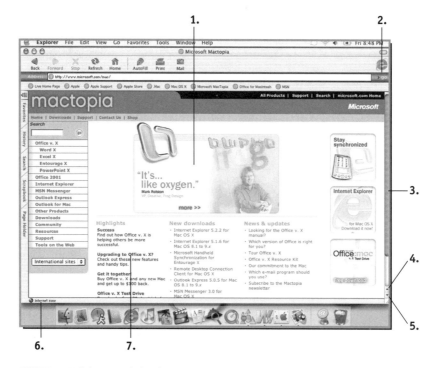

FIGURE 29. Web browser window features.

1. **Browsing window.** This is the area where Web pages are displayed.

2. **Go button.** When a Web site address is typed in the address window, clicking the Go button takes you to the site.

3. **Scroll bar.** Click and drag the box here to move up or down the page displayed in the browsing window.

4. **Scroll-up arrow.** Click on this arrow to scroll up the page displayed in the browsing window.

5. **Scroll-down arrow.** Click on this arrow to scroll down the page displayed in the browsing window.

6. **Connectivity icon.** When you see this icon, it indicates that you are online.

7. **Link.** Links are very powerful. They enable you to move from one Web page to another. Links appear as text or graphics. To find a link, move your cursor across the browsing window. Whenever the cursor changes to a hand icon, it is pointing at a link. Text links are usually easy to identify because the text will be a different color. To access a link and view additional pages, click when the hand icon appears.

Understanding Web site addresses

The anatomy of a Web site address

Before learning more about browser tools, it's important to understand the structure of Web site addresses, or URLs. This is because you use the browser tools in conjunction with Web site addresses you enter into the address bar. Web site addresses are often confusing to work with if you don't understand the naming conventions.

VOCABULARY TERMS

URL

An abbreviation for Uniform Resource Locator. Every file on the Internet has a unique address, or URL, assigned to it so you can find the file. URLs have two parts. The first part identifies the protocol or format of the file. Web page URLs usually begin with "http." The second part of the URL is the domain name, which identifies where the Web page you want is stored.

domain name

A domain name is part of an Internet address or URL.

Let's take a closer look at an actual URL (Figure 30):

FIGURE 30. Sample URL.

1. **Protocol.** This identifies the format of the file you are accessing. Most Web pages begin with http://. There are two other protocols you may encounter.

   - **https://** indicates a secure Web site where steps have been taken to protect data.

   - **ftp://** means file transfer protocol and indicates that a file has been uploaded on an ftp server. This file can be downloaded in full by a computer that accesses the ftp address.

Parts 2–4 comprise the domain name. Here's what each part means:

2. **www.** This stands for World Wide Web. Most, but not all, URLs include this.

3. **Host.** This identifies the owner of the Web site. In the example above, "ISTE" tells you that the International Society for Technology in Education owns the Web site.

4. **Domain suffix.** This part of the URL is very important because it provides information about the origin of a Web page. You can use this information to help determine the credibility of a Web page. There are a limited number of suffixes. The most common are:

   - **gov**   government

   - **edu**   education

   - **org**   organization

   - **com**   commercial

   - **net**   network

   - **mil**   military

The domain suffix of **org** in the sample URL tells you that ISTE is an organization.

How can you use this information to determine site credibility? Look at the two imaginary Internet addresses below:

   - http://www.excellentuniversity.edu

   - http://www.excellentuniversity.com

Which address is more likely to be legitimate? Probably the address ending in **edu**, because this tells you it is an educational institution. The address ending in **com** tells you this is a commercial site.

Many of the URLs you find in this directory will have additional information beyond the domain suffix. This is because the address through the suffix takes you to the Web site home page. The additional information will take you further into the site, bypassing the home page. For example, the URL **http://www.census.gov/govs/www/school.html** takes you beyond the home page for the Census Bureau (http://www.census.gov), directly to a document titled *Federal, State, and Local Governments Public Elementary-Secondary Education Finance Data.*

Entering a URL

To enter a new URL, you must first clear the URL already in the address bar. Do this by pointing at the URL in the address bar and clicking once. This will highlight the existing URL (Figure 31).

FIGURE 31. Highlighting an existing URL.

When the existing URL is highlighted, you can begin typing the new Web address. Be very careful as you type the address. Include all punctuation marks and check the spelling. The URL must be entered exactly to successfully access the Web site.

If you make a mistake, you can click once to highlight the text in the address bar and begin over. You can also correct an error by pointing at the mistake and clicking twice. This causes a flashing cursor to appear in the address bar where you have pointed. You can then edit the URL by using the delete key and retyping. Editing a URL uses the same techniques you use to edit in a word-processing document.

Once the URL is correctly typed, press Enter or click on the Go button to access the new Web site (Figure 32).

FIGURE 32. Go button.

You need to wait for the Web page to download before you can read it. This is when the speed of your connection becomes important. A dial-up connection takes much longer to download a site, especially if there are many graphics.

Occasionally you will have difficulty opening a Web page. You may see a message saying that the page cannot be displayed. Check to make sure you typed the URL correctly. If you made a mistake, retype or edit the URL and try again. If the URL appears to be correct, it's possible that the site is temporarily down, that the URL has been changed, or that the page is no longer available. Wait awhile and try the URL again. If you continue to get the error message, read and follow the directions that appear with the message. They will take you to the site's home page, where you may be able to find the specific information you need.

Essential Web browser tools

Now that you have opened a Web page, you need to know about the tools you can use to navigate the site and save or print information. Look closely at Figure 33. You see eight tool buttons here. Although you may want to learn more about all the buttons on this bar, to get started you really only need to use three: Back, Forward, and Print.

FIGURE 33. Essential Web browser tools.

Back and Forward

A common experience for new Internet users is to follow several links in a Web site and suddenly become "lost," not understanding how to retrace their steps to return to a previous page. There are several ways to move back and forth between pages you've visited using the Back and Forward buttons.

The simplest way to go back and forth is to move page by page. You can do this by clicking on the Back or Forward buttons. Each click moves one page forward or backward, depending on which button you choose (Figure 34).

FIGURE 34. Back and Forward buttons.

The appearance of the buttons tells you whether there are pages to move to. For example, in Figure 34, the Back button is dark blue and the label is in black text (active), indicating there are Web pages that can be moved back to, but the shadowy appearance (inactive) of the Forward arrow and label indicates there are no pages currently to move forward to. Therefore, at this time the Web page displayed is the last page visited during this session.

Print

There are times you will want to print a site page instead of making it a Favorite. Perhaps you want specific information but doubt that you would want to visit the site again at a later time. Printing the Web page that is currently in the browsing window is easy. Simply click on the Print button in the toolbar (Figure 35).

FIGURE 35. Print button on toolbar.

Favorites

You will find Web sites that you want to revisit at a later time. This means you cannot access them from the Back and Forward drop-down menus because these include only those sites accessed during the current online session. You could keep a hand-written list of sites next to your computer, but then you would need to worry about copying URLs accurately and not losing the list!

Fortunately, Web browsers provide an option that allows you to make a list of sites you want to go back to later. Some browsers call this "bookmarking," but in Internet Explorer it's called "Favorites." By clicking on the tab labeled Favorites on the left side of the screen, you open a column on the left side of your browser window (Figure 36). There is a button here that allows you to add a site to the list. You can also scroll through the list, highlight the name of a site, and click. This takes you directly to that site.

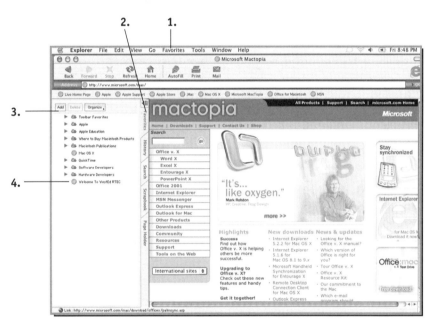

FIGURE 36. Using Favorites tools.

1. **Favorites menu.** Click here to see a drop-down menu that allows you to work with Favorites without opening the box on the left side of your screen.

2. **Favorites tab.** This tab acts like a toggle switch. Click it once and the Favorites list will appear on the left side of your screen. Click it again, and the Favorites list will be hidden.

3. **Add button.** When you are visiting a site you'd like to add to your Favorites list, click on this button and the site will appear in your Favorites list.

4. **Favorites list.** This is the list of sites you can save and visit time after time. Most browsers come installed with certain sites already included in the list.

COMMON PROBLEMS ENCOUNTERED BY BEGINNERS

CONNECTION ISSUES

Problem

You're using a new computer and a fast modem, but the dial-up connection is sometimes sluggish.

Remedy

Even with top-of-the-line equipment, if you use a dial-up connection, you may be logged on to the Internet at a speed far slower than your equipment can handle. When connecting to the Internet using a dial-up connection and an ISP account, watch as the connection is made to see what the connection speed is. If it is less than 49,333 bps, disconnect and try again.

Problem

Your computer is frequently disconnected from the ISP while browsing Web pages or trying to work online.

Remedy

You are most likely using an older computer and modem and/or a dial-up connection. If your equipment is more than three years old, talk with a technician about upgrading or replacing it. Although data transmission is slower over a dial-up computer, newer computers and modems can generally handle graphics-intensive Web sites without being disconnected.

NAVIGATION ISSUES

Problem

"The page cannot be displayed" error message appears on your screen when trying to access a Web page.

Remedy

Here are four things to try:

1. Check the spelling and punctuation in the URL. Common mistakes include extra letters (wwww instead of www, for example) or missing periods or slash marks. Edit the URL and click Go again.

2. If the URL is correct, the Web site may be down temporarily. Try to access the site later.

3. If the URL is correct, the Web site may have been revised. The error message provides the option of clicking on the site's Home page URL. Click on this and look at the Home page to try to locate a link that will take you to the information you want.

4. If you click on the Home page URL provided on the error page and cannot enter the site, the site may be temporarily down or it may no longer exist.

NAVIGATION ISSUES

Problem

You have used links to visit several pages and want to go back to a previous page, but the Back button is not active.

Remedy

Some Web pages actually open a new browser window when accessed. If you cannot use the Back button to retrace your steps, click on the black 'X' in the upper right corner of the open window (upper left corner on a Mac). This will close the extra browser window and, in effect, take you back one page where the Back button should be active.

Problem

You have used links to visit several pages and want to go back to a previous page. The Back button is active, but when you click on it, you don't move back to the previous page.

Remedy

This is called "mousetrapping." There are sites that intentionally try to make it difficult for you to use the Back button to leave the site. Usually you can go back by being persistent and clicking the mouse several times. If this doesn't work, you may need to type in a URL and press Enter or click Go to leave.

FAVORITES ISSUES

Problem

You've added a home page to your Favorites but can't find the specific link you wanted within the site.

Remedy

When you want to return to a particular place in a Web site at a later time, you can add that specific page to your list of Favorites by clicking the Add button when you are viewing that page. Home pages of Web sites that are frequently updated may not continue to feature a specific link, and it can be very difficult to retrace your steps later.

Problem

You've developed a lengthy list of Favorites, but the titles they're saved under mean nothing to you, so you don't remember which is which.

Remedy

When you add a site to your Favorites list, it will appear as the last title in the list. You can highlight the name, right click one time, and select Rename from the drop-down menu that appears. You can then give the site a name that will be more meaningful to you later.

Problem

Today at school you added a site to your list of Favorites, but it doesn't appear on your Favorites list on your computer at home.

Remedy

You will not be able to access a list of Favorites stored on one computer from any other computer. If you find a site at school that you want to work with at home (or anywhere else), the easiest way to handle it is to add the site to your Favorites list and then either write down the URL or copy and paste it into a word-processing document. You can then e-mail the word-processing file to yourself and retrieve it at home. There are other solutions, but they require more advanced Internet skills. See Tips and Tricks for More Experienced Internet Users.

UNWANTED DOWNLOADS

Problem

You open a Web page and see a message stating that you must download a program to properly view a site.

Remedy

Think before you download this kind of program. First, if you do it at the office you may be violating download policies. Second, if it happens at home you can quickly clutter your hard drive with programs you don't need. Third, some of these programs actually upload information about your Internet surfing habits to commercial businesses. Finally, this can be a way that a virus or other harmful program can be introduced to your computer. So, you may miss out on an occasional extraordinary site, but it's worth it in order to avoid more serious problems.

As you increase your Internet use, you may want to talk with your district's technician to find out which of these programs are OK for downloading.

CHAPTER 3

Beyond the Basics

N ow that you have Internet basics under your belt, you may be perfectly content to stick with what you know, and that's great. However, if you find yourself thinking, "There must be another way to get where I want to be on the Internet," you're in the right place. This chapter explains how to circumvent some limitations of certain browsers, work with more than one Internet window simultaneously, organize your Favorites, and conduct your own searches on the Internet.

USING MULTIPLE BROWSERS

Even after you've established a means for connecting to the Internet and have selected an Internet service provider (ISP), there may be times when you choose to use one browser over another, and it's not uncommon to find several different browser programs preinstalled on a computer's hard drive, for instance, Internet Explorer, Netscape Communicator, and America Online (AOL).

Accessing the Internet from multiple computer systems or locations may create a need to use more than one browser. For example, if you have a DSL connection, you might use Internet Explorer as the default browser. However, when traveling, DSL may not be available. A paid account for a national ISP such as AOL enables you to make a toll-free dial-up connection almost everywhere you might go.

Another reason to use multiple browsers is that some sites work better with one browser than with another. For example, a site page that shows lots of white space and requires much scrolling to see everything on a page when viewed using Netscape may look just fine in Internet Explorer. The opposite also happens; a page that looks funny in Internet Explorer will be quite readable in Netscape. How will you know when the browser makes a difference?

Often the site's home page will clearly state: "This site best viewed using ..." and then will name the preferred browser(s). Other times, you find out through trial and error. If the spacing on a page doesn't seem to make sense or if the graphics aren't clear, try switching browsers. If you are using a DSL or other high-speed connection where your computer is Internet-connected whenever it's on, simply close the browser you're currently using and double-click on the icon for the browser you'd like to open. Of course, to use AOL or another subscription service, you must have a paid account to use the proprietary browser.

Speaking of AOL, many users mistakenly think their ability to access or use certain sites is limited because they use AOL. (Some sites state "This feature not available to AOL users.") That may be true if you try to go through AOL's Internet browser, but you have an alternative. Once you have signed on and made your online connection, minimize the AOL browser window (Figure 1 for Windows, Figure 2 for Macintosh) so you can see your Desktop. You still have the Internet connection established and can open Internet Explorer or Netscape and use one of these browsers to access sites.

Minimize button

FIGURE 1. To maintain your connection and see your Desktop, click on the Minimize button.

Minimize button

FIGURE 2. Finding the minimize button on a Macintosh using AOL.

If you want to return to AOL, simply click on the AOL icon in the menu bar at the bottom of your screen (Figure 3 for Windows, Figure 4 for Macintosh).

AOL Icon

FIGURE 3. To view the AOL window again, click on the icon in the menu bar.

AOL Icon

FIGURE 4. Finding the AOL icon on a Macintosh menu bar.

USING MULTIPLE WINDOWS

There are times when you may want to have more than one Internet site open at a time. Perhaps you want to flip back and forth to compare content, or you are using information from one site to complete an online form on another site. It's much more efficient to do this using more than one window rather than using the Back and Forward tools.

Opening a second window is easy (Figure 5). Click on File on the menu bar. Scroll to New and click on Window. The window you see will be a duplicate of the one you had open when you executed the new window command. Once you've opened another window, you can enter a new URL as usual. This works in both Windows and Macintosh environments.

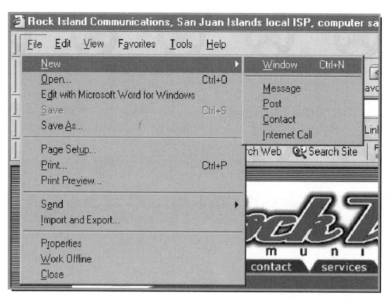

FIGURE 5. Opening a new window.

In a Windows environment, moving back and forth between browser and other types of open windows is also easy (Figure 6). You look at the menu bar at the bottom of your screen. The buttons in the center portion indicate currently open files. The small icon at the left of each title tells you what kind of file (i.e., Word, Internet Explorer) each is. To move back and forth between Internet files, click on the buttons labeled with the Internet Explorer icon.

You can also move between Internet files and other documents such as a word-processing file. Look at Figure 6. Between the two Internet Explorer buttons is a button with a Word icon at the left of the title. To switch to the word-processing document, click once on that button.

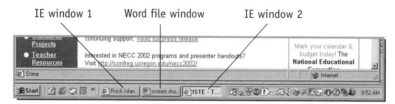

FIGURE 6. Here you see two buttons for Internet Explorer windows and one for a Word window. Open a window by clicking on its button.

You can move between programs on a Macintosh by clicking on the various program icons in the toolbar on the Desktop (Figure 7).

FIGURE 7. Toolbar icons for QuickTime, Word 2001, and AOL.

Although the Windows environment also allows users to tile windows on the screen so that you can see two or more simultaneously (Figure 8), most people seem to prefer the method shown in Figure 6 because the images quickly become too small to read easily and more scrolling is required to see everything on a page. The Macintosh environment does not allow tiling except within certain programs, such as AppleWorks.

To access the Tile Windows commands, point your cursor at the gray area to the right of the menu bar at the bottom of your screen. Right-click once, scroll to either Tile Windows Horizontally or Tile Windows Vertically, and click again. Every currently open file will be displayed in a window. To return to viewing just one window, right-click in the gray area again and select the Undo Tile option that appears.

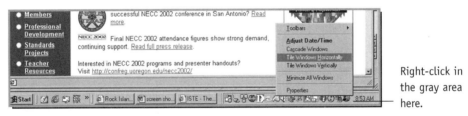

Right-click in the gray area here.

FIGURE 8. Accessing the Tile Windows commands.

ORGANIZING YOUR FAVORITES

After a period of time, you may find that you have added so many bookmarks that your list is quite lengthy and you can't remember what a particular bookmark is or why you saved it. To avoid confusion, you can set up file folders for your Favorites, just like you set up folders for word-processing and other files you want to keep. You do this by using the Organize Favorites box, which can be accessed from the Favorites button on the main toolbar (Figure 9) or from the Favorites panel (Figure 10).

Favorites button

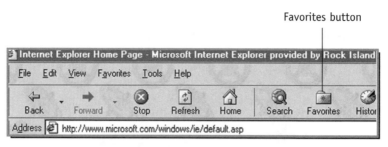

FIGURE 9. Favorites button.

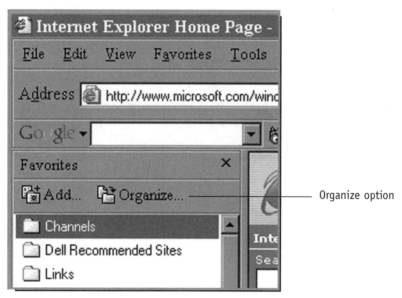

Organize option

FIGURE 10. Favorites panel.

Remember, when using a Macintosh, you access Favorites on the commands menu at the top of the screen or by clicking on the Favorites tab at the left of the screen. Both methods offer Organize options.

Creating a new folder

Open your Favorites panel, then position your cursor over the Organize button, and click once again. Figure 11 shows the Organize Favorites box in a Windows environment. Figure 12 shows Macintosh.

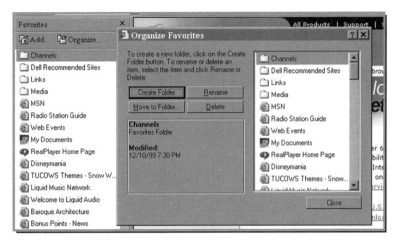

FIGURE 11. Organize Favorites box on a PC.

FIGURE 12. Organizing Favorites box on a Macintosh.

To create a new folder, place the cursor over the Create Folder button and click once. If in a Windows environment, a new folder then appears in the list to the right. Type a name for the folder and press the Enter key. When using a Macintosh, the new folder will appear in the Favorite list to the left. You may also create folders within folders. To do this, click on a folder in the list on the right (Windows) or left (Macintosh). Now click Create Folder and name the folder as directed above.

To move a Favorite

To move a Favorite into a folder or from one folder to another when in a Windows environment, find the name of the Favorite in the list to the right. If the Favorite is already in a folder, you will need to click on the name of that folder to see the list of the Favorites currently stored within the folder. Highlight the Favorite name by clicking on it once. Now click on the Move to Folder button (Figure 11). The Browse for Folder window will appear (Figure 13).

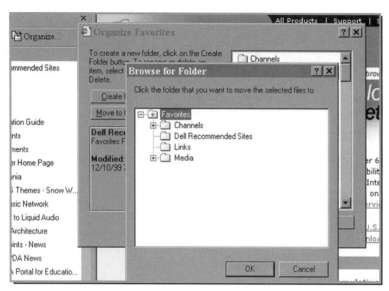

FIGURE 13. Browse for Folder window.

Navigate to the folder where you want to place the Favorite. To open a folder, double click on the folder. Click once on a folder to select it. Once the folder is selected, click OK to move the Favorite into the selected folder.

In a Macintosh environment, look at your Favorites list, highlight the name of the Favorite you want to move, and drag it to the folder where you want it placed.

To delete a Favorite

You may find that you no longer want to have a site included in your Favorites list. To delete a Favorite in a Windows environment, use the Favorites list on the right to locate it (Figure 11). Place the cursor over the name on the Favorite you want to delete and click once to highlight the name. Then click once on the Delete button. Click once on Yes in the Confirm File Delete box that appears. The Favorite then disappears from the list.

In a Macintosh environment, look at your Favorites list, highlight the name of the Favorite you want to delete, and click on the Delete button next to Add and Organize.

Renaming a Favorite

Often when adding a site to Favorites, the name that appears in the Favorites list makes little or no sense in terms of remembering later what the site might be. You can easily rename Favorites to something that can help nudge your memory later when searching for a particular Favorite.

To rename a Favorite in a Windows environment, place the cursor over the name on the Favorite you want to rename and click once to highlight the name. Then click once on the Rename button (Figure 11). The name of the Favorite is now highlighted in an Edit box (Figure 14). Now you can type the new name for the Favorite and press the Enter key.

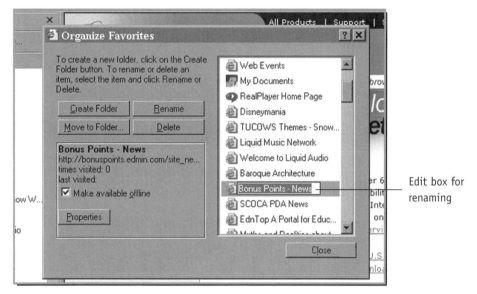

FIGURE 14. Edit box for renaming a Favorite.

In a Macintosh environment, look at your Favorites list, highlight the name of the Favorite you want to rename, and type the new name.

To close the Organize box

When you are finished organizing your Favorites, click once on the Close button (Windows) or the Favorites tab (Macintosh).

CONDUCTING SUCCESSFUL SEARCHES

Many Internet users love to surf the Web, moving from site to site looking for interesting pages. If you happen to have a lot of time on your hands and don't need to find something specific quickly, it can be fun to poke around and see what you come up with. However, most of us can't afford to spend that kind of time on the off chance we might find something. Using a Web directory or a search engine can help point your searches in the right direction and ensure that your time online is well spent.

VOCABULARY TERMS

search engine

A program that searches files for specified key words and produces a list of files where the key words are found. Although this term refers to a type of program, people are generally referring to programs such as Google, Alta Vista, or Excite, which are used to search for files on the World Wide Web.

Web directory

A list of categories and subcategories you can browse to find Web sites. It is most helpful when you're looking for general information.

Web directories

Some popular Web directories include WebCrawler (**www.webcrawler.com/info.wbcrwl/**) and Yahoo! (**www.yahoo.com**). Figure 15 shows a directory listing from Yahoo! To use a directory, simply choose a category and click on it to see the subcategories within it. You can trace the categories and subcategories you've moved through by referring to the bar near the top of the screen, which shows the title of each category and subcategory you have accessed (Figure 16). A Web directory can be a useful tool when you have a general topic in mind but aren't certain of exactly what it is you're looking for. For instance, you may want to look at some examples of school Web sites but don't have particular schools you want to see. Yahoo!'s Web directory allows you to go to an area called Schools, where you can select grade levels; then to states where the schools are located; and finally to a list of schools that have Web sites in the state you specify.

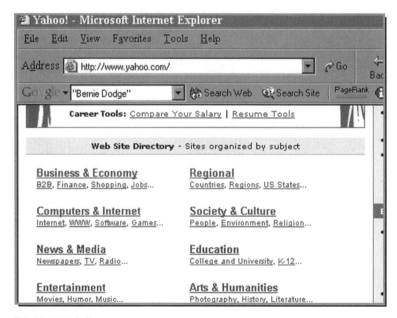

FIGURE 15. Web directory.

Category   Subcategories

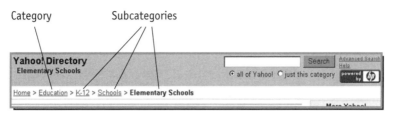

FIGURE 16. Tracing the steps taken in a search using a Web directory.

Search engines

When you do have a specific topic or item you need to find, such as an online article, it is best to use a search engine. Search engines search an index of Web pages looking for keywords you enter in a text box. Each search engine uses its own index, so you will find different results using different engines.

Some of the more popular search engines include Google (**www.google.com**), Alta Vista (**www.altavista.com**), and Lycos (**www.lycos.com**). Figure 17 shows a search results page for a search done using Google.

Results are shown as hyperlinks. Click on the title to access the Web site.

Advanced Search features may be accessed here to improve your searching techniques.

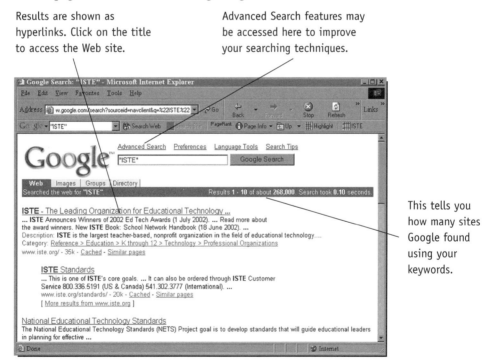

This tells you how many sites Google found using your keywords.

FIGURE 17. Google search results page.

Searching for sites can be frustrating if you simply rely on using keywords without knowing a few tricks to use along the way. Bernie Dodge, Ph.D., is a professor of educational technology at San Diego State University. He works with educators who are learning to use the Internet and has developed what he calls "Four NETS for Better Searching." (Here, NETS is an acronym for the four steps you take when searching and should not be confused with the ISTE-sponsored NETS project, which focuses on student, teacher, and administrator technology standards.) These four tips are some of the best around, and Dr. Dodge has graciously agreed to allow them to be listed here for you. They are based on the Google search engine.

1. **Start Narrow:** Search engines allow you to identify words you want included in your search, as well as words you don't want to include. For example, click on the Advanced Search option of Google, where you can define keywords in the following categories:

   • with **all** the words

   • with **any** of the words

   • **without** the words

   This is helpful when conducting a search for a particular person, place, or thing that may share its name with multiple others. If you want to find Washington Elementary School in a city in Florida rather than every Washington Elementary School across the country, you can use the name of the city and state to narrow the search.

2. **Find Exact Phrases:** When you enter multiple keywords, the results will list every site in the search engine's database with the words together or individually. Thus, if you search using the keywords "elementary school," you'll get all occurrences of the words collectively and individually. That may be okay until you start finding results that quote Sherlock Holmes ("Elementary, my dear Watson.") rather than sites related to elementary schools. Search engines allow you to indicate that you only want sites that include the *exact phrase* you are using as keywords.

3. **Trim Back the URL:** You may find an interesting site in a search that has a long URL. For example, suppose you've discovered a resource for research at **http://www.iste.org/research/caret.html**. You may think the site could offer additional information elsewhere. Trim the URL by leaving off the last portion after the final backslash: **http://www.iste.org/research/**. Trim once again by typing **http://www.iste.org**. This technique can also work when you receive a message that a particular page is no longer available. Trimming the URL may help you find the page at a new location within the site.

4. **Look for Similar Pages:** Look at Figure 17. Each Web site listed in Results has a hyperlink called Similar Pages. By clicking on this link, you can access additional pages Google identifies as having content much like the page listed.

You can read more about the "Four NETS for Better Searching" and run through some search practice exercises by visiting **http://webquest.sdsu.edu/searching/fournets.htm**. Once you are comfortable using the advanced search options with Google, explore the advanced options with another search engine, such as Alta Vista or Lycos.

National Educational Technology Standards for Administrators (NETS•A)

All school administrators should be prepared to meet the following standards and performance indicators. These standards are a national consensus among educational stakeholders of what best indicates effective school leadership for comprehensive and appropriate use of technology in schools.

I. Leadership and Vision

Educational leaders inspire a shared vision for comprehensive integration of technology and foster an environment and culture conducive to the realization of that vision. Educational leaders:

A. facilitate the shared development by all stakeholders of a vision for technology use and widely communicate that vision.

B. maintain an inclusive and cohesive process to develop, implement, and monitor a dynamic, long-range, and systemic technology plan to achieve the vision.

C. foster and nurture a culture of responsible risk-taking and advocate policies promoting continuous innovation with technology.

D. use data in making leadership decisions.

E. advocate for research-based effective practices in use of technology.

F. advocate, on the state and national levels, for policies, programs, and funding opportunities that support implementation of the district technology plan.

II. Learning and Teaching

Educational leaders ensure that curricular design, instructional strategies, and learning environments integrate appropriate technologies to maximize learning and teaching. Educational leaders:

A. identify, use, evaluate, and promote appropriate technologies to enhance and support instruction and standards-based curriculum leading to high levels of student achievement.

B. facilitate and support collaborative technology-enriched learning environments conducive to innovation for improved learning.

C. provide for learner-centered environments that use technology to meet the individual and diverse needs of learners.

D. facilitate the use of technologies to support and enhance instructional methods that develop higher-level thinking, decision-making, and problem-solving skills.

E. provide for and ensure that faculty and staff take advantage of quality professional learning opportunities for improved learning and teaching with technology.

III. Productivity and Professional Practice

Educational leaders apply technology to enhance their professional practice and to increase their own productivity and that of others. Educational leaders:

A. model the routine, intentional, and effective use of technology.

B. employ technology for communication and collaboration among colleagues, staff, parents, students, and the larger community.

C. create and participate in learning communities that stimulate, nurture, and support faculty and staff in using technology for improved productivity.

D. engage in sustained, job-related professional learning using technology resources.

E. maintain awareness of emerging technologies and their potential uses in education.

F. use technology to advance organizational improvement.

IV. Support, Management, and Operations

Educational leaders ensure the integration of technology to support productive systems for learning and administration. Educational leaders:

A. develop, implement, and monitor policies and guidelines to ensure compatibility of technologies.

B. implement and use integrated technology-based management and operations systems.

C. allocate financial and human resources to ensure complete and sustained implementation of the technology plan.

D. integrate strategic plans, technology plans, and other improvement plans and policies to align efforts and leverage resources.

E. implement procedures to drive continuous improvements of technology systems and to support technology replacement cycles.

V. Assessment and Evaluation

Educational leaders use technology to plan and implement comprehensive systems of effective assessment and evaluation. Educational leaders:

A. use multiple methods to assess and evaluate appropriate uses of technology resources for learning, communication, and productivity.

B. use technology to collect and analyze data, interpret results, and communicate findings to improve instructional practice and student learning.

C. assess staff knowledge, skills, and performance in using technology and use results to facilitate quality professional development and to inform personnel decisions.

D. use technology to assess, evaluate, and manage administrative and operational systems.

VI. Social, Legal, and Ethical Issues

Educational leaders understand the social, legal, and ethical issues related to technology and model responsible decision-making related to these issues. Educational leaders:

A. ensure equity of access to technology resources that enable and empower all learners and educators.

B. identify, communicate, model, and enforce social, legal, and ethical practices to promote responsible use of technology.

C. promote and enforce privacy, security, and online safety related to the use of technology.

D. promote and enforce environmentally safe and healthy practices in the use of technology.

E. participate in the development of policies that clearly enforce copyright law and assign ownership of intellectual property developed with district resources.

This material was originally produced as a project of the Technology Standards for School Administrators Collaborative.

APPENDIX B

Correlation to NETS•A

The full text of the National Educational Technology Standards for Administrators (NETS•A) and individual performance indicators is provided in Appendix A. District leaders who are engaged in coursework for credentialing or professional growth may, as part of their work, be required to develop and implement action plans based on the standards. Every site listed in the directory of Internet sites includes information that can be used in conjunction with implementation of one or more of the performance indicators.

In some instances, as part of their own evaluation process, district leaders are asked to develop professional growth plans, including work in the area of instructional technology. Again, the sites listed in the directory provide resources and materials that can be used in developing and implementing this type of plan.

The tables in this appendix are designed to facilitate professional growth plan development. Each table reflects one section of the directory, and every Web site in that section is listed. Next to each Web site name and URL is a matrix that indicates which of the NETS•A standards are related to the primary areas of emphasis in that site.

NETS•A CORRELATION MATRIX: BUSINESS

NAME OF SITE/INTERNET ADDRESS	STANDARDS					
	I. LEADERSHIP & VISION	II. LEARNING & TEACHING	III. PRODUCTIVITY & PROFESSIONAL PRACTICE	IV. SUPPORT, MANAGEMENT, & OPERATIONS	V. ASSESSMENT & EVALUATION	VI. SOCIAL, LEGAL, & ETHICAL ISSUES
FACILITIES/INFRASTRUCTURE:						
Council of Educational Facility Planners, International (CEFPI) www.cefpi.com	▓			▓		
DesignShare http://designshare.com				▓		
Indoor Air—IAQ Tools for Schools www.epa.gov/iaq/schools				▓		▓
National Clearinghouse for Educational Facilities (NCEF) www.edfacilities.org				▓		▓
NetDayCompass.org www.netdaycompass.org				▓		
School Planning and Management Magazine www.peterli.com/spm/				▓		▓
Universal Service Administrative Company www.sl.universalservice.org				▓		
FINANCE:						
Association of School Business Officials International (ASBO) http://asbointl.org	▓			▓		
Education Finance Statistics Center http://nces.ed.gov/edfin				▓		
Federal, State, and Local Governments: Public Elementary-Secondary Finance Data www.census.gov/govs/www/school.html				▓		
Office of the Chief Financial Officer: U.S. Department of Education www.ed.gov/about/offices/list/ocfo/				▓		
Taking TCO to the Classroom http://classroomtco.cosn.org	▓			▓		

NETS•A CORRELATION MATRIX: BUSINESS

NAME OF SITE/INTERNET ADDRESS	STANDARDS					
	I. LEADERSHIP & VISION	II. LEARNING & TEACHING	III. PRODUCTIVITY & PROFESSIONAL PRACTICE	IV. SUPPORT, MANAGEMENT, & OPERATIONS	V. ASSESSMENT & EVALUATION	VI. SOCIAL, LEGAL, & ETHICAL ISSUES
FOOD SERVICES:						
American Diabetes Association **www.diabetes.org**		▓				▓
American School Food Service Association (ASFSA) **www.asfsa.org**	▓			▓		
National Dairy Council **www.nationaldairycouncil.org**		▓				
National School Lunch Program **www.fns.usda.gov/cnd/Lunch/**				▓		
PURCHASING:						
National Association of Education Buyers (NAEB) **www.naeb.org/membership.htm**	▓			▓		
U.S. Communities: Government Purchasing Alliance **www.uscommunities.org**				▓		
TRANSPORTATION:						
National School Transportation Association (NSTA) **www.yellowbuses.org**	▓			▓		
School-Bus.org **www.school-bus.org/Home_Links/Gateway.htm**				▓		▓
School Transportation News **www.stnonline.com**				▓		▓

NETS•A CORRELATION MATRIX: EDUCATIONAL SERVICES

NAME OF SITE/INTERNET ADDRESS	**STANDARDS**					
	I. LEADERSHIP & VISION	II. LEARNING & TEACHING	III. PRODUCTIVITY & PROFESSIONAL PRACTICE	IV. SUPPORT, MANAGEMENT, & OPERATIONS	V. ASSESSMENT & EVALUATION	VI. SOCIAL, LEGAL, & ETHICAL ISSUES
BILINGUAL EDUCATION:						
National Association for Bilingual Education (NABE) www.nabe.org	■	■				
National Clearinghouse for English Language Acquisition and Language Instruction Educational Programs (NCELA) www.ncela.gwu.edu		■				
Office of English Language Acquisition, Language Enhancement, and Academic Achievement for Limited English Proficient Students (OELA) www.ed.gov/about/offices/list/oela/		■			■	
Portraits of Success www2.lab.brown.edu/NABE/portraits.taf		■				
CURRICULUM AND INSTRUCTION:						
Association for Supervision and Curriculum Development (ASCD) www.ascd.org	■	■			■	
Content Knowledge—3rd Edition www.mcrel.org/standards-benchmarks		■				
Exploration in Learning and Instruction: The Theory Into Practice Database http://tip.psychology.org		■				
Federal Resources for Educational Excellence (FREE) www.ed.gov/free		■				

NETS•A CORRELATION MATRIX: EDUCATIONAL SERVICES

NAME OF SITE/INTERNET ADDRESS	STANDARDS					
	I. LEADERSHIP & VISION	II. LEARNING & TEACHING	III. PRODUCTIVITY & PROFESSIONAL PRACTICE	IV. SUPPORT, MANAGEMENT, & OPERATIONS	V. ASSESSMENT & EVALUATION	VI. SOCIAL, LEGAL, & ETHICAL ISSUES
EARLY CHILDHOOD EDUCATION:						
Everything for Early Childhood Education: EduPuppy **www.edupuppy.com**		■				
National Association for Education of Young Children (NAEYC) **www.naeyc.org**	■	■				
Technology in Early Childhood Education **www.netc.org/earlyconnections**		■				
GRANT WRITING:						
Getting Grants: Finding Funding Sources Online **www.libraryspot.com/features/ grantsfeature.html**				■		
Grantionary **www.eduplace.com/grants/help/grantionary.html**				■		
Grants and Contracts **www.ed.gov/fund/landng.jhtml**				■		
SchoolGrants **www.schoolgrants.org**				■		
PUPIL PERSONNEL:						
The Behavior Home Page **www.state.ky.us/agencies/behave/ homepage.html**						■
National School Public Relations Association (NSPRA) **www.nspra.org**	■					■
Office of Safe and Drug-Free Schools (OSDFS) **www.ed.gov/about/offices/list/osdfs/**						■
The SafetyZone **www.safetyzone.org**						■
School Safety **www.nea.org/issues/safescho**						■

NETS•A CORRELATION MATRIX: EDUCATIONAL SERVICES

NAME OF SITE/INTERNET ADDRESS	I. LEADERSHIP & VISION	II. LEARNING & TEACHING	III. PRODUCTIVITY & PROFESSIONAL PRACTICE	IV. SUPPORT, MANAGEMENT, & OPERATIONS	V. ASSESSMENT & EVALUATION	VI. SOCIAL, LEGAL, & ETHICAL ISSUES
SPECIAL EDUCATION:						
Center for Applied Special Technology (CAST) www.cast.org		■				■
Council for Exceptional Children (CEC) www.cec.sped.org	■					■
National Center for Learning Disabilities www.ncld.org		■				■
SchwabLearning.org www.schwablearning.org		■				■
SPECIAL PROJECTS:						
Especially for Parents www.ed.gov/parents/landing/jhtml?src=pn		■	■			
National PTA www.pta.org	■					
No Child Left Behind www.ed.gov/nclb/landing.jhtml		■	■		■	
Office of Vocational and Adult Education (OVAE) www.ed.gov/about/offices/list/ovae		■	■			
Regional Educational Laboratories Network www.relnetwork.org	■	■	■		■	■
Student Achievement and School Accountability Programs www.ed.gov/about/offices/list/oese/sasa					■	
TECHNOLOGY:						
Center for Applied Research in Educational Technology (CARET) http://caret.iste.org		■			■	■
eSchoolNews Online www.eschoolnews.com	■	■	■	■	■	■

NETS•A CORRELATION MATRIX: EDUCATIONAL SERVICES

NAME OF SITE/INTERNET ADDRESS	STANDARDS					
	I. LEADERSHIP & VISION	II. LEARNING & TEACHING	III. PRODUCTIVITY & PROFESSIONAL PRACTICE	IV. SUPPORT, MANAGEMENT, & OPERATIONS	V. ASSESSMENT & EVALUATION	VI. SOCIAL, LEGAL, & ETHICAL ISSUES
International Society for Technology in Education www.iste.org	X	X	X	X	X	X
Network of Regional Technology in Education Consortia (R*TEC) www.rtec.org	X	X	X	X	X	X
Planning for Technology: Putting the Pieces Together www.edgateway.net/cs/tk/print/rtec_docs/tk_home.html	X	X				X
Technology Briefs for NCLB Planners www.neirtec.org/products/techbriefs/	X	X				X
Technology Information Center for Administrative Leadership (TICAL) www.portical.org	X	X	X	X	X	X
TESTING, ASSESSMENT, AND RESEARCH:						
Brown Center on Educational Policy www.brookings.edu/browncenter	X				X	
National Assessment Governing Board (NAGB) www.nagb.org	X				X	
National Center for Educational Statistics (NCES) http://nces.ed.gov/practitioners/administrators.asp	X				X	
National Center for Research on Evaluation, Standards, and Student Testing (CRESST) www.cse.ucla.edu	X				X	
Rand Education www.rand.org/education/	X				X	

NETS•A CORRELATION MATRIX: GENERAL

NAME OF SITE/INTERNET ADDRESS	STANDARDS					
	I. LEADERSHIP & VISION	II. LEARNING & TEACHING	III. PRODUCTIVITY & PROFESSIONAL PRACTICE	IV. SUPPORT, MANAGEMENT, & OPERATIONS	V. ASSESSMENT & EVALUATION	VI. SOCIAL, LEGAL, & ETHICAL ISSUES
Education Commission of the States www.ecs.org	■	■		■	■	
Education Week on the Web www.edweek.org	■	■	■	■	■	■
Fed World www.fedworld.gov		■		■		■
SmartBrief www.smartbrief.com/ascd	■	■		■	■	■
U.S. Department of Education www.ed.gov	■	■	■	■	■	■

NETS•A CORRELATION MATRIX: PERSONAL PRODUCTIVITY

NAME OF SITE/INTERNET ADDRESS	STANDARDS					
	I. LEADERSHIP & VISION	II. LEARNING & TEACHING	III. PRODUCTIVITY & PROFESSIONAL PRACTICE	IV. SUPPORT, MANAGEMENT, & OPERATIONS	V. ASSESSMENT & EVALUATION	VI. SOCIAL, LEGAL, & ETHICAL ISSUES
Add-A-Form www.addaform.com			▓		▓	
Adobe Acrobat Reader www.adobe.com/products/acrobat/ readstep2.html			▓			
Backflip www.backflip.com			▓			
Education Online for Computer Software www.educationonlineforcomputers.com			▓			
Tripod www.tripod.lycos.com			▓			

NETS•A CORRELATION MATRIX: PERSONNEL

NAME OF SITE/INTERNET ADDRESS	STANDARDS					
	I. LEADERSHIP & VISION	II. LEARNING & TEACHING	III. PRODUCTIVITY & PROFESSIONAL PRACTICE	IV. SUPPORT, MANAGEMENT, & OPERATIONS	V. ASSESSMENT & EVALUATION	VI. SOCIAL, LEGAL, & ETHICAL ISSUES
HUMAN RESOURCES:						
American Association of School Personnel Administrators (AASPA) **www.aaspa.com**	▓					
Electronic Privacy Information Center (EPIC) **www.epic.org**						▓
Social Security Online **www.ssa.gov**						▓
U.S. Department of Labor: Bureau of Labor Statistics (BLS) **www.bls.gov**					▓	
U.S. Equal Employment Opportunity Commission (EEOC) **www.eeoc.gov**						▓
PROFESSIONAL DEVELOPMENT:						
e-Lead: Leadership for Student Learning **www.e-lead.org**		▓			▓	
National Staff Development Council (NSDC) **www.nsdc.org**	▓	▓			▓	
TEACHER QUALITY:						
ERIC Clearinghouse on Teaching and Teacher Education **www.ericsp.org/pages/about/index.html**		▓			▓	
National Board for Professional Teaching Standards (NBPTS) **www.nbpts.org**		▓			▓	
National Governors Association: Teacher Quality **www.nga.org/center/topics/1,1188,D_401,00.html**		▓				
Teacher Evaluation: New Directions and Practices **www.teacherevaluation.net**					▓	
Teacher Evaluation Kit: Glossary **http://www.wmich.edu/evalctr/ess/glossary**					▓	

NETS•A CORRELATION MATRIX: SOCIAL, LEGAL, AND ETHICAL ISSUES

NAME OF SITE/INTERNET ADDRESS	STANDARDS					
	I. LEADERSHIP & VISION	II. LEARNING & TEACHING	III. PRODUCTIVITY & PROFESSIONAL PRACTICE	IV. SUPPORT, MANAGEMENT, & OPERATIONS	V. ASSESSMENT & EVALUATION	VI. SOCIAL, LEGAL, & ETHICAL ISSUES
Copyright and Fair Use, Stanford University Libraries **http://fairuse.stanford.edu**						■
Education Law Association **www.educationlaw.org/links.htm**						■
FindLaw **www.findlaw.com**						■
IDEAPractices **www.ideapractices.org**						■
Markkula Center for Applied Ethics, Santa Clara University **www.scu.edu/ethics**						■
Public Education Network (PEN) **www.publiceducation.org**		■			■	■

NETS•A CORRELATION MATRIX: SUPERINTENDENT'S OFFICE

NAME OF SITE/INTERNET ADDRESS	STANDARDS					
	I. LEADERSHIP & VISION	II. LEARNING & TEACHING	III. PRODUCTIVITY & PROFESSIONAL PRACTICE	IV. SUPPORT, MANAGEMENT, & OPERATIONS	V. ASSESSMENT & EVALUATION	VI. SOCIAL, LEGAL, & ETHICAL ISSUES
ADVOCACY:						
Federal Register www.gpoaccess.gov/fr/	■					■
THOMAS: Legislative Information on the Internet http://thomas.loc.gov	■					■
U.S. Department of Education Mailing Lists www.ed.gov/MailingLists/	■					■
LEADERSHIP:						
American Association of School Administrators (AASA) www.aasa.org	■					
Clearinghouse on Educational Policy and Management (CEPM) www.cepm.ed.gov	■					
Council of the Great City Schools www.cgcs.org	■					
District Administration www.districtadministration.com	■					
WORKING WITH BOARDS OF EDUCATION:						
Improving School Board Decision Making: The Data Connection www.schoolboarddata.org	■		■		■	
National Association of State Boards of Education (NASBE) www.nasbe.org	■					
National School Boards Association (NSBA) www.nsba.org	■					

Glossary

Techies are a lot like educators when it comes to vocabulary: they tend to use many acronyms and terms nontechnology users don't recognize. One hurdle to becoming a proficient Internet user is simply learning the language. The following glossary includes the basic terms used in chapters 1–3.

cable modem. A modem designed to send and receive data through television cable networks. Data transmission speed is very fast, but the technology is still being refined. Not available in all areas through all cable companies.

domain name. A domain name is part of an Internet address, or URL. The number of domains is limited, and they provide an important clue to the origin of a Web page. Educators need this information to help determine the credibility of a Web page. The common domains you encounter are:

gov	government
edu	education
org	organization
com	commercial
net	network
mil	military

How can you use this information? Look at the two imaginary Internet addresses below.

http://www.excellentuniversity.edu

http://www.excellentuniversity.com

Which address is more likely to be legitimate? Probably the address ending in edu, because this tells you it is an educational institution. The address ending in com tells you this is a commercial site.

DSL. Short for digital subscriber lines. DSL offers subscribers a high-speed Internet connection through telephone lines. DSL is not available in all areas and is dependent upon subscribers' proximity to telephone switching stations.

home page. The main page of a Web site.

Internet. The Internet provides the network infrastructure that enables millions of computers around the world to connect to one another for communication purposes.

ISP. Short for Internet service provider. These companies provide access to the Internet for a monthly fee. A dial-up connection to the Internet requires that a user go through an ISP to access the Internet.

modem. Stands for **mo**dulator-**dem**odulator. This device may be external (outside your computer) or internal (usually a card plugged into a slot inside your computer). The modem converts data stored on your computer into a format that can be transferred via telephone or cable lines. Different modems send and receive data at different speeds. Generally, the faster the better.

search engine. A program that searches files for specified keywords and produces a list of files where the keywords are found. Although this term refers to a type of program, people are generally referring to programs such as Google, Alta Vista, or Excite, which are used to search for files on the World Wide Web.

URL. An abbreviation for Uniform Resource Locator. Every file on the Internet has a unique address, or URL, assigned to it so that you can find the file. URLs have two parts. The first part identifies the protocol, or format, of the file. Web page URLs begin with the letters http. The second part of the URL is the domain name, which identifies where the Web page you want is stored.

For example, to find the International Society for Technology in Education, the URL is **http://www.iste.org.**

The domain name provides important information about the kind of site you are viewing (see definition for *domain name*).

Web browser. This is a software application (program) used to access Web pages. The two most commonly used Web browsers are Internet Explorer and Netscape Navigator.

Web directory. A list of categories and subcategories you can browse to find Web sites. It is most helpful when you're looking for general information.

World Wide Web. The World Wide Web is one source of information for Internet users, but it is not the Internet itself. It uses the Internet network to allow people to access Web sites.